Life without

The quiet revolution

Written by

Veronika Sophia Robinson
Eliza Serena Robinson
Bethany A. Robinson
Paul Robinson

February 25, 2010

♡

Dearest Wendy ♡

May our stories
augment your own family's
journey through the "education"
years. Brightest blessings

Veronika
xo

Paul Eliza

Bethany

Life Without School: the quiet revolution
© 2010 Veronika Sophia Robinson, Paul Robinson,
Bethany A. Robinson, Eliza Serena Robinson

ISBN 978-0-9560344-2-7

Published by Starflower Press
www.starflowerpress.com

Cover photograph of Bethany and Eliza Robinson by
Paul Robinson: *music practice on the village green.*
Photographs on pages 62, 70, 200, 204 and 205 by David Hollins.

British Library Cataloguing in Publication Data.
A catalogue record for this book is available from the British Library.

Other books by Veronika Robinson, published by Starflower Press:
The Drinks Are On Me: everything your mother never told you about
breastfeeding
The Birthkeepers: reclaiming an ancient tradition
Stretch Marks: selected articles from The Mother magazine
2002 – 2009 (co-edited with Paul Robinson)

Also by Veronika:
The Compassionate Years (a history of the Royal New Zealand
Society for the Prevention of Animals)
Fields of Lavender (poetry)
Contributing poet in Howl at the Moon
(published by Wild Women Press)

*"Unschooling is like ambling along
on a relaxed Sunday afternoon,
smelling the flowers,
and hearing the insects as they fly about doing their work.*

*Anything else is like driving along in a racing car
in order to reach the finish line,
with no time to take in the surroundings."*

~ Veronika Sophia Robinson

Veronika's Dedication

For *Paul*, my soul's love: who unfailingly stands shoulder to shoulder with me in our parenting, love, business and life. Thank you for being the life partner of my dreams, and an ideal father to our daughters.

For *Bethany*, my first born. May you continue to blossom, and never be afraid to share your talents with the world. You have so very much to give. I can't imagine my life without you or your sister.

For *Eliza*, those almond eyes and your contagious laughter give meaning to everything I do. I know that all those years of "I can't sleep" weren't just to wind me up, but because you really *did* want to know what's at the end of forever.

Note: *I've used extracts from The Mother magazine's unschooling column, and some of my editorials. These are not necessarily in chronological order. Apologies if you're a long term reader of The Mother, for the repetition. I chose them because they were written in the moment, and provide an honest reflection of our life at the time. In many ways, they're like diary entries. I trust you'll enjoy re-reading them.*

Disclaimer: *This book is not intended to be a text or tome on unschooling or home education ~ it's a picture into our life, and is intended to provide insights, and hopefully inspiration, to those who are called to travel through life with their family in a similar way.*

"Unschooling" is a term coined by the late educator and author, John Holt. When I use the term 'radical unschooling', it's not to be confused with a book of that title which encourages absolutely no rules or boundaries in parenting children.

Bethany's Dedication

For my family.

Eliza's Dedication

For the two fluffy things (cats), and to new friends I'm yet to meet. For my sisters Hannah, Harriet and Bethany, Mum and Dad, and my Grandmother.

Paul's Dedication

For my dear *Veronika*, my life's love, who has inspired me, opened my eyes, helped draw out the best in me, and with whom I've flourished as never before.

My *four daughters*, for everything they've taught me, and continue to teach me.

When I was at school, in the olden days, we had a very boring series of first readers, called Janet and John. Nearly 60 years later, I owe a lot to another Janet and John ~ neither of whom I've met.

I bumped into *Janet Kennedy*, a wonderful, generous, conscious, questioning soul, on an Internet spiritual forum. Were it not for her guidance and friendship, I doubt if I'd be where I am now, spiritually (wherever that is!).

John Sherman is a teacher whose simple but profound message has changed many lives for the better.

The Robinson family, Autumn 2001

Thank You!

A heartfelt thank you to *Siobhán Kramer, Keeley Farrington, Angela and Jonathan Henry* for reading through the draft manuscript. Thank you so much for your honest feedback, input and caring thoughts.

Derek Robinson of Bluebell Bookshop: for everything! Your unique place and generous spirit have allowed authors, artists, astrologers, poets, knitters and musicians to share their talents with the community.

Your beautiful community space has provided a foundation for our unschooling life. Within the heart of Penrith, my family has gathered in a world of books, raspberry scones and the best fluffy hot chocolates in the world. You've graciously opened up your business as a sanctuary within the town centre. It's our first stop for books, and the sofas have our names on them.

Derek, you've always welcomed my feisty little girls, even when they were noisy toddlers who raced up the stairs to get to the glorious children's area. You've offered up your shop as a resource centre for our learning, and that's priceless. Thank you for always being so enthusiastic about my magazines and books, and for willingly stocking them.

Your nurturing has not gone unnoticed, my friend, and we pray that you're richly rewarded for the gifts you've shared in this lifetime.

Karen Arnott for being such a wonderful Web Mother ~ the words "thank you" don't conjure up the depth of feeling associated with our continuing gratitude. Thank you so much for being part of our life's work. www.arnottdesign.co.uk

Simon Marston ~ is there a chocolate factory big enough to create what you're worth in cacao beans? Hardly! For the past eight years you've provided such a support to my techno-dunce ways. Rest assured, I don't take you for granted, and will happily ply you with chocolate, pizza…whatever it takes, to have you be my right hand techno-boy. Thank you so very much for helping me to get my 'print ready' books and magazines *truly* print ready.

And to those who've helped nurture our health and well-being over the years: *Madhu Bhana* (cranio-sacral therapist in Auckland, New Zealand); *Harriet Wood* (homeopath in Penrith, Cumbria); and *Christophe Vever* (chiropractor in Carlisle, Cumbria) ~ THANK YOU!

Our daughters ~ *Bethany* and *Eliza* ~ for teaching us!

Contents

Teaching

From The Prophet, by Kahlil Gibran

*Then said a teacher, Speak to us of Teaching. And he said:
No man can reveal to you aught but that which already lies
half asleep in the dawning of your knowledge. The teacher who
walks in the shadow of the temple, among his followers, gives
not of his wisdom, but rather of his father and his lovingness.*

*If he is indeed wise, he does not bid you enter the house of his
wisdom, but rather leads you to the threshold of your own
mind.*

*The astronomer may speak to you of his understanding of space,
but he cannot give you his understanding.*

*The musician may sing to you of the rhythm which is in all
space, but he cannot give you the ear which arrests the rhythm,
nor the voice that echoes it.*

*And he who is versed in the science of numbers can tell of the
regions of weight and measure, but he cannot conduct you
thither.*

*For the vision of one man lends not its wings to another man.
And even as each one of you stands alone in God's knowledge,
so must each one of you be alone in his knowledge of God, and
his understanding of the Earth.*

Foreword

The seed of this book was conceived in my childhood ~ a time of life with school ~ 13 long, and mostly boring, years of school. The gestation of the written word began life in 2006, when I was invited to speak at the *Irish Home Educators' Network Annual Conference* because of my role as editor of The Mother magazine, a publication which champions, amongst other things, human-scale education.

Although I felt honoured at the invitation, I must admit to feeling like a fraud! What could I possibly talk about when we 'don't do anything all day'? The temptation to go to Ireland as a family that Autumn was too much to resist. It also meant the opportunity to visit our beautiful friends who live off-grid in County Meath ~ as well as travelling to County Wicklow, where the conference was held, in an area of natural beauty.

As I began to write down my thoughts on our life as an unschooling family, it dawned on me that there was so much I could share, and not to be fooled by the simplicity of our lifestyle. It's very easy to take one's way of life for granted, and not to appreciate what a revolution it might be for another family if they were to embark on a similar journey. From that invitation to Ireland, this book grew. It wasn't until Winter, 2008, that I began to put this book together, and we, as a family, completed *Life Without School* the following Winter. This turning of the year seemed a very symbolic gestation. It gave us, and the book, time to grow, and to feel each season of Nature as we reflected on all our years together.

This book could equally have been titled *The Heart*. If I was to sum up unschooling in one word, it would be 'love'. Love for our children, love for freedom, love for learning, love for life.

Veronika Sophia Robinson
Glassonby, Eden Valley, Cumbria
January 2010

"The heart is the hub of all sacred places.
Go there and roam in it."
Sri Nityananda.

Part One
by Veronika Sophia Robinson

Bethany and Eliza celebrate Spring.

Introduction

Life Without School is a scrapbook of my family's memories: snapshots of our life. If you can imagine this book as a patchwork quilt full of different ideas and images, in no particular order, yet all sewn together, you'll get a picture of our unschooling life.

It's 8pm on a deep, dark and snowy December evening in 2008. I'm perched just inches from the wood fire, writing up notes for this book. Bethany is knitting a Christmas gift beneath the light of the lamp, a cat snoozing upon her lap. Eliza, deep in thought, is writing a story about a home-educated girl; and Paul is reading. On the piano rests a piece of music called *Tingalya* that Eliza composed earlier in the day in honour of a Sun Goddess she'd created during her story writing.

Such a scene couldn't be further removed from what most people consider to be education, and yet, here, by the hearth of our home, lies the heart of our family's journey of home education. And these are the moments I love and cherish, and will always hold dearly in my heart. It's scenes like this that I want to share with the world; scenes which show that learning can be fun, peaceful, harmonious and family-based ~ and not led by so-called 'experts', but by the children themselves.

Have you ever walked into a bookshop and seen the number of autobiographies written by people who've barely started out on life? There was a time when autobiographies were written once a person had finished their career, and had had time to reflect on their life's journey. Not these days. It seems anyone and everyone can write an autobiography, even while still in their teens. It doesn't sit comfortably with the traditionalist in me; and yet, I feel by writing this book, I'm a bit like a teen sharing her life story.

My daughters, Bethany and Eliza, haven't finished their 'school' years by any means, and yet we feel there's so much to tell. It seems that the time is right to share the first part of our journey into this still relatively unexplored way of choosing to educate children. How different our story will be in five years time is anybody's guess. We certainly can't predict what paths we'll take, individually, or as a family unit; however, it's been said that the best way to predict the future is to create it, and that's certainly what we're doing.

This book has no pretensions about being an unschooling manual or a 'how to' guide, of any description. It's simply our family's journey ~ what works, and what doesn't work for us; what we love, and what we're not so keen on. You won't find lesson plans: we have none, although we've tried such artificial learning devices. There's no curriculum upon which Bethany and Eliza's education is based. To provide any sort of advice or 'how to' book would defeat the purpose. What we hope to do is open the door to our tiny sandstone cottage in the heart of rural Cumbria, and invite you to sit with us by the fire, and share our stories. When Spring arrives, you might like to hike up to the woods, or down by the Eden River to dip your toes. In Summer, you'll learn where the best gooseberries, raspberries and wild cherries grow, and, together, we'll stand for hours foraging and chatting. By Autumn, the crab apples might tempt you to make jelly, or a wreath with apples and rosehips to adorn the mantelpiece as a seasonal celebration. By Winter, more of your time may be spent indoors, yet you'll need to help chop wood to make the home warm, and heat the water when the frost bites.

Living in Cumbria, England, I've discovered the seasons to be short and sharp ~ unlike my childhood in Australia. Every season brings its own rhythm into our home; and each one reminds us that, in many ways, there are more than four seasons, for each ebbs and wanes, and has such a life of its own, with contrasts and contradictions. Our seasonal experiences include traditions, rituals, animal-free recipes, natural healing modalities, and celebrations. We hope you enjoy them.

On any given day, during any season of the year, you'll find each of us engaged in our own activities. Sometimes they'll be shared ones, like cleaning, or preparing vegetable beds for planting, or painting a room. In the kitchen, someone might be making soup, while another is playing violin or piano. Another may be singing or composing, and someone else playing dolls. Amongst the aromas and sounds, an invisible energy swirls through the house. Each day it grows stronger and builds upon itself. This is the essence of our unschooling journey. It's called life, and the resounding message of this book is that *life* is an education.

One of the most important things I've learnt about unschooling, is from being an Attachment Parent. The influence of Jean Liedloff's book, *The Continuum Concept*, has shaped our lives enormously. Our girls were raised in-arms, like the Yequanna Indians of South America. This means they were carried in a sling all day long against our chests, and slept in our bed at night. They were carried constantly until they were ready to crawl, and then they were carried whenever they needed or wanted to beyond that time, well into toddlerhood. A child raised this way sees us living *our* life. We're not on the floor watching the baby live *her* life. How boring that would be for the baby! Right from the beginning, the girls were intimately involved in the jobs we were doing: whether in the kitchen preparing a meal; hanging laundry; weeding the garden; mowing the lawn (motorless mower); enjoying long walks; going to see a live concert; shopping; visiting friends; swimming.

As toddlers, this theme continued. By seeing Paul and I live our lives with passion, the girls learnt to imitate this in their play. Now, as adolescents, I see how clearly this modelling has shaped their lives. Their passions aren't the same as ours, yet they've benefitted enormously from having us simply get on with our lives, rather than being child-centred.

Our style of home education is commonly called 'unschooling'. We seek to let the children be autonomous in how they learn, rather than to force education with a curriculum, timetable or agenda (hidden, or otherwise) for when and how things are learned.

The Slow Movement has gained popularity as a way of bringing more consciousness into day-to-day life. Slow Food is not only about cooking or creating your own meals from scratch, but choosing to use slow ingredients, such as locally grown organic and biodynamic produce, and fruits and vegetables which you've grown yourself.

I feel unschooling is very much part of the Slow Movement. We seek an organic approach, and bring consciousness to our days. We avoid rush, where possible, and find meaning in each moment. At the heart of this journey is trust. We trust that our children will learn everything that is relevant to their life, and that they'll do so because they want to learn it, rather than having had it forced upon them. I also feel this is one of the fundamental differences between families who choose home education rather than unschooling. As a rule, home educators tend to actively fill their days with outings and activities to 'ensure' plenty of learning happens. An unschooler knows that learning happens, regardless of what you plan or where you are.

Amongst the aromas and sounds,
an invisible energy swirls
through the house.

Each day it grows stronger
and builds upon itself.

This is the essence
of our home education journey.

It's called life...

My Friend Bluey

"Coercion or compulsion never brings growth.
It is freedom that accelerates evolution."
~ Paramahansa Yogananda, Autobiography of a Yogi.

I was born in the city of Brisbane some 40 plus years ago, and grew up on a property in South East Queensland, Australia. My first school was a suburban one in Brisbane, but, a year later, I sat in a tiny country school in rural Australia with twenty six children and two teachers.

My main memories of Freestone State Primary School are of my lovely young teacher romantically kissing her husband, on the wooden verandah; and the fear I felt every time I had to go to the toilet, for it was an outdoor one at the other end of the school field, and was without lighting or a flushing loo, and not nearly so civilised as the modern day compost loo. The toilets, or 'dunnies' as we called them, had very long holes in the ground. We covered our poo with sawdust. Apart from the stench of the loo, I was always scared of meeting a red-belly black snake as I ran for my life across the school field. Every trip to the toilet was traumatic.

I was bullied right from the beginning. The girls in class would tell me I was getting my words wrong, and that words like 'thin' were really 'thick', etc. After a few years, and enough bullying to last a child a lifetime, my parents took me from Freestone to a town school ~ Warwick East Primary School. Things weren't much better. My victim mentality followed me to town and into that school, and the secondary school ~ Warwick State High School ~ when I was a teenager.

At ten years old, I took off from an inter-school sports competition with about five boys from my class. We were heading down to the river for a swim on that hot Summer's day. The Condamine River runs through the Rose and Rodeo town of Warwick, and provided a great play area for 'wagging' school children like myself, who wanted to be well out of view of adults. On the way there, however, the boys stopped to talk to a truck driver who'd broken down. What is it about boys and vehicles? He was waiting for the repair man to come and see to his lorry. The driver was in his late fifties, and had a head of wiry ginger hair. His face was smattered with freckles, and his light blue eyes twinkled like starlight. I instantly liked him, and we recognised each other as soul friends. Eventually, after much chat, he asked permission to read my palm. I was thrilled. Apart from my mother, I never had anyone else I could talk to about the more esoteric aspects of life.

The boys did head off to the river, but I stayed behind, talking to my new friend, Bluey. I'd met a kindred spirit, and our friendship lasted for the rest of his life. We kept in touch by letter, and he also came out to meet my family to calm any fears they might've had about me befriending an older man. As it turned out, ours was a friendship which spanned three countries and twenty five years. Tears still come to my eyes when I think about that fateful day, and how if I'd been a 'good girl' and stayed at sports day, I may never have met my very dear soul-friend, Bluey. Even if it had been a regular school day, I wouldn't have met him (unless, of course, it was on one of the countless other days that I 'wagged' school). An interesting side note is that even when I was ten, Bluey saw on my palm that one day I would give birth to a 'big' daughter. Eliza was born ten pounds and four ounces. She likes to say to me, "Ten pounds and four ounces, at your service!"

Bluey moved back to New Zealand. When I was twenty-three I went over to visit him, and ended up living in New Zealand for eight years. We also met in England when we both went off travelling. He lived an unusual life ~ sometimes living in a truck, at other times a cave. We shared a deep interest in spiritual matters, and I'm honoured to have had a friendship with him that also included my life as a child. When he died, his daughter told me that he still had all the things I'd made him during my childhood, such as an embroidered pillowcase with his name on, and lots of poetry and letters.

Bluey was one of the highlights of my school years! My other highlights involved the days I had *off* school, staying at home with my Mum. We lived in subtropical Queensland, and grew bananas, paypaya, olives and avocados in the garden. Sometimes my Mum would say to me that I could have the day off school if I wanted. I didn't even have to pretend that I was sick. That was magic to my little ears, because I really disliked school. I was constantly bullied, and found the lessons a chore. They were neither inspiring, nor relevant to my life. As one of eight children, one on one time with my Mum was a real treat and not something to be missed. I still value the times we had together. They're the days I remember, not the days when we were all in the house, or my lessons at school. My fondest school memories were when we went on school camps to remote locations, but they usually only happened about once a year. Definitely not worth going to school for! By secondary school, my mother had me exempted from sport afternoons (thank you, thank you, thank you!), and I attended sessions at the Theosophical Society, learning about the more esoteric aspects of life. It was such a joy in my week to explore topics that I was passionate about. I learnt to read auras, and understand about chakras and healing.

I do believe I learnt far more from being with my mother than I ever learnt in school. Those years, inside school buildings, felt like such a waste. The tests, the grades ~ none of them showed who I *really* was; how I felt; how I thought; what was important to me. I wasn't stupid, but school somehow made me feel inadequate. It wasn't a place which allowed me to shine. What it did do, though, was put labels on me which were an inaccurate picture of the abilities, talents, insights, joys and the beauty within my heart and soul. They crippled me, and attempted to steal my essential self. The one message that I remember strongly from school was that I was voted by most teachers as the student 'least likely to succeed in life'. Charming!

My mother, on the other hand, was able to plant seeds in my mind, which funnily enough, may not have manifested for another two decades, but they certainly have shaped my life. I've learnt more about this world, and how to live happily in it, from my mother, than from 13 years of schooling.

When my younger brother, Kamahl, and sister, Ramona, came of school age, my mother decided not to send them to school, but to educate them using the Australian Correspondence School Course. Together they would sit in the sunshine doing lessons. I was so envious! Their style of home education meant recreating school in the home, and is completely the opposite from that which happens with Bethany and Eliza. I remember feeling, though, that they were so lucky being able to stay home with Mum. Their activities looked fun (or more fun than what I was doing in school), but it was a full-time job for my Mum, who was running a property of several hundred acres while my Dad worked overseas for months and years on end. Something had to give. They did eventually go to school, but I have no doubt that the extra time they had at home helped to preserve their self-esteem.

My friend, Bluey, in New Zealand.

Those feelings I had when I went to school, while my siblings were enveloped in the warmth of the family home, stayed with me. Twenty years before becoming a mother, I promised my future children that they wouldn't be forced to go to school.

My dear friend Bluey clearly came into my life for a reason. He believed in me in a way that no school teacher ever did. He repeatedly told me that I had a strong 'destiny line' on my palm, and promised me that my life held real purpose.

In my last year of formal education, the teachers were trying to define me, my learning style, and what sort of course I should continue with for further education. The best definition they could come up with was 'hybrid'. It was meaningless to me at the time, and as it happened, I left formal education until I was 23 and enrolled in correspondence University courses. That didn't last either ~ so boring!

I can see now that, like Eliza, I like to absorb information from a wide variety of sources, and to put my own definition onto subjects. My interests aren't limited to one or two topics, but are vast and broad. The subjects I do wish to specialise in are pursued in ways that are meaningful to me, and draw on a wide variety of experts, rather than a set curriculum. I imagine it will always be like this for me.

The Good, The Bad and The Snugly

Winter 2004/2005 ~ The Mother magazine, Issue 12

I'm often asked, "What's it like being with your children all the time?"

The good of unschooling

Imagine the bliss of waking up with your lover, both of you naked and warm beneath the sheets, on a bitterly cold Winter morning. You've woken at your leisure, and have time to luxuriate in each other's touch. You laugh, chat; and indulge in eye contact. Life feels good. Life is slow. When we're in slow time, we're in bliss time. Life has meaning in these moments.

Unschooling mornings: the day is still dark. My kids are reading books, snuggled up in bed. When we're ready, we'll bathe, have breakfast, and make our way to the warmth of the open fire. I'll light some geranium incense, and play music. We'll talk about what the day might bring, about what each member of the family might like to do, or indeed needs to do. We'll bake, read, sew, play the piano. Perhaps some friends will come for lunch, or we'll visit someone. To me, our gentle start to the day has the same pace as my above analogy. The day is our own.

I've not had to fight the clock to get the children into uniforms, and packed lunches made, or to brave the elements to take my girls to the bus stop. As their day goes on, I'm intimately involved in their expression of life. I'm aware of their feelings, and am there to witness their moments of joy and frustration in their self-initiated endeavours.

The bad of unschooling

Now, love him as I do, He Who Shares The Duvet has been known to snore (but only till I tickle him). He's also known to pull the duvet just that bit too far, leaving me and my red tartan pyjamas victim to the bitter chill in the room. I'm exposed.

My kids are a bit like HWSTD. They find my weak spot, my rawness, my wounds. And they'll pull at my psychological duvet until there's nothing left of the thing, or me. They've mastered the art of uncovering me.

The thing about being with your children all the time is that you're not trying to artificially condense life into some pre-ordained package called quality time. It's a myth perpetuated by people who refuse to recognise that children are creatures of the moment, asking questions when the need to know arises, and not at 10am on Saturday because that's when mum or dad has scheduled to spend time with them.

The snugly of unschooling

The questions Eliza asks: "Where does petrol come from? Why is it bad for the Earth? How did the Earth begin?" (Big Bang explained as a possible theory.) "But how does anyone *know* that no-one was there? Are all planets round?" Her most ardent questions come first thing in the morning, before I've even put a foot out of bed, before my brain has engaged. I find this difficult. Yet I find it more difficult to think she probably wouldn't get the opportunity to ask even half the questions (let alone have them answered) if she were in a school environment.

Eliza was in my bed last night. My eyes were shut. I was just about to fall asleep, when a very assertive voice asked, "What's gravity?"

"Eliza," I moaned. I answered dutifully, but my answer wasn't enough for her. "Does it make you fall over? Is it real?" I felt exasperated. Where are all these questions coming from?

"Mum, does anything grow on the Moon? How many days does it take to get there?"

Today she's onto the evolution of humans. "Will we ever see an ape give birth to a human?" And then she wants to know why she doesn't know very much!

After discovering the real reason why I don't want to live in Australia, Eliza has become obsessed, to say the least, with snake questions ~ looking for her mother's raw spot, and watching her wince: "How does a snake laugh? Do water snakes eat rice? Why do snakes hibernate?"

I can only begin to imagine what the next decade of parenting will be like.

Within the last few weeks, Eliza's reading has really taken off. She's ever so pleased with herself now that she can read chapter books on her own. I wake to the sound of Eliza laughing out loud, just as Bethany did when she first started reading. This morning, Eliza waltzed down the staircase, pleased as punch for having just read two chapters. I overheard the commentary she was giving to her Unseen Audience: "And she loved reading so much, she forgot about how many other things she had to do in her busy life…"

It took me straight back to when I was her age, stuck up the Magic Faraway Tree, and hearing my mother in the distance asking me to set the table for dinner. Hearing her, but not quite able to come down.

Eliza at Lake Ullswater, Cumbria.

Her most ardent questions come first thing in the morning,
before I've even put a foot out of bed,
before my brain has engaged.
I find this difficult.

Yet I find it more difficult to think she probably wouldn't
get the opportunity to ask even half the questions
(let alone get them answered)
if she were in a school environment.

Top left: Veronika at 16, when formal education ended. And three years later, in the late eighties when perms and Laura Ashley style dresses were 'in', working at the Hills Montessori School, Adelaide, in South Australia.

My Early Years

The Springtime of my life began with kindergarten in sub-tropical Queensland. What should have been such tender, innocent years, playing beneath banana trees, were laced with an insidious distrust of 'authority'. One of the adults, into whose care I was entrusted, sexually abused me. When my mother addressed this with the person in charge of the kindergarten, it was dismissed very matter-of-factly: "That sort of thing doesn't happen here!" It was here that I learnt to falsely believe that my most sacred, feminine self could be discarded and disposed of secretly ~ that it had no value in my life; indeed, that it was something to be ashamed of or hidden away. I also learnt that my feelings, thoughts and opinions meant nothing in the world of education. Sadly, it was also the start ~ the trigger point ~ of many other men magnetically being drawn to 'abuse and violate' me throughout my childhood, and into early adulthood. We can't ever underestimate the impact of violating another person's trust.

As a young adult, I had the pleasure of working in Montessori kindergartens/schools, and seeing early childhood education in a new way. These small schools were places of love, beauty, reverence and care, and although I wasn't aware of it at the time, I'm sure it was integral to healing my belief pattern that 'men are bastards' and that 'childhood isn't safe'. One of the songs we taught the children was about being aware of their body: *"My body's nobody's body but mine. You run your own body, let me run mine."* It helped heal me, and showed me that I could set up clear boundaries in my relationships.

When I was a child, I learnt to read the starry sky as a map, and make shelter on the mountains where we lived. I would ride my horse for hours, and go camping without a tent; light a fire; and cook my food.

I've tried really hard to remember my school lessons, but what I do remember from childhood came from life ~ foals being born, rescuing a joey, a crow and other birds on our property in rural Australia.

I remember kittens born in my bed; eating tomato soup outside with my Mum; sleeping on the trampoline at night with her; picking wild mushrooms in the rain for the best soup you've ever had. When my Dad wasn't working overseas, I helped him build fences, break-in horses; and I climbed trees.

My school memories aren't so rosy: there was relentless bullying about my little nose, my German name, my mosquito-bitten legs ("scabby legs"), my German parents, that I wasn't Catholic, my vegetarian diet ("You'll die if you don't eat meat!"), that I didn't know the Top Ten songs in the charts, and that my favourite record was Perry Como's Christmas album. While the other students did talks on rock bands, I spoke about reincarnation.

Sticks and stones can break my bones,
but names will never hurt me.

"It's not true. Names do hurt, don't they?"

Charles Ingalls to his daughter, Mary, when she was bullied at school. Little House on the Prairie.

Bethany and Eliza, dancing in the wild flowers, learning about fun, dance and relationships.

Why Did We Choose Home Education?

Before I conceived my daughters, I knew in my heart that I wouldn't send them to school. At that time, my reasons were based purely on my childhood experience of being bullied and misunderstood. How I got through my school years with *any* self-esteem is beyond me. By secondary school, girls were dunking my head down the toilet, threatening to beat me up after school because I didn't shave my legs (I was always more scared of missing the school bus, as we lived a long way from town), and generally making my day-to-day life hell.

One thing was for sure, I wasn't conceiving my children consciously, and raising them in-arms, only to toss them into institutional learning led by those who had no real interest in them. History was not going to repeat itself.

As it turned out, my husband had also been severely bullied in school. It was inevitable that, between us both, home-education was the best option for our much loved children.

Although bullying is still a factor in our unschooling choice, it doesn't come at the top of the list any more, because the girls are old enough to speak their minds. Our reasons are many and varied, but primarily we want our children to enjoy their childhood, to discover who they are and what they love to do, in a space and place of relative freedom, but primarily, a space of love. We want them to find an inner discipline, and to identify themselves in ways that aren't about how much they scored in a test, or who their friends are.

People in our culture have been indoctrinated to believe that children learn in school, and have to be force-fed certain bits of important information, at certain times, with children of their own age ~ and to then regurgitate that information at the right time. If such a belief is so strongly reinforced in a culture, it takes an enormous amount of courage to break from the ranks. It can seem as if you're directly attacking someone else's choice by saying your children don't go to school. I'm always surprised by how many people consider it a challenge to their lifestyle, as if they have to justify their choice. It's also interesting how people feel they have the right to criticise the home education choice ~ because, if it was the other way around, they certainly wouldn't like it.

Bethany and Veronika, exploring a lake's edge in Cumbria.

The Quiet Revolution

"The Mother's heart is the child's school room."
~ Henry Ward Beecher

Life without school is a quiet revolution. Child-led, spontaneous learning is how our ancestors and ancestresses have learned throughout time, so we shouldn't be surprised by this turn of the wheel. Autonomous learning is nothing new.

The revolution that's occurring now is that, family by family, we're waking up to the Great School Swindle: the false idea that children must attend school to learn, and that only 'experts' can teach them.

The revolution isn't being witnessed on television screens. It's not visible (yet) through mass protests on the streets, where families are demanding their civil right to raise their children as Nature intended. It wouldn't surprise me, though, if such a sight was seen in the not too distant future. We're seeing so many other liberties being eroded. Theoretical legal structures are in place which will impact on parents' rights to refuse vaccination, as well as how home educated children will be 'monitored' by the state.

At the time of writing, the UK government is seeking to implement changes which will violate families and their educational freedoms.

Unschooling begins from birth. It's a way of life, and doesn't suddenly begin at 4, 5, 6 or 7, as in formal, structured education. Our children are always learning, and so are we. Most of what we ever learn in life we learn in our first few years anyway, so it makes the idea of sending our children off to someone else to learn seem rather nonsensical.

My children don't have a regimented lifestyle, and because we do many activities together and/or spend much of our time together, they have an extremely rich environment for learning.

Unschooling is still relatively unheard of, but this quiet revolution is very likely to generate more interest in the mainstream, especially while governments around the Western world exert more pressure and control on children and their families, and their liberties. Forget about home education being the preserve of the fringe element, it's not. It's being adopted by more and more people from all walks of life, who understand that children really *want* to learn, and, when left alone by adults, get pretty excited by life and learning.

Given the choice between autonomous education and formal learning, many parents are beginning to see that their children's lives can be better, real, wholesome, honest, uncompromised, and most important of all: enjoyable.

Unschooling is as simple as allowing your child to stay away from school, and giving them the freedom to explore the world in which they live. The role of an unschooling parent is not to control the child, or to dictate the 'how' of learning. It's a lifestyle, rather than a method of home-education. We allow our children to learn about life from the world around them, without being confined in a school building, or come to that, in their home. We choose not to force a curriculum upon them. The children choose their subjects, and the time and space in which to learn them. And they do this from the earliest age.

Their learning isn't aligned to a timetable any more than it's pitched against a set of goals. Unschooling allows each child to trust in their ability to find a path of learning which reflects their uniqueness, creativity, interest, curiosity and spontaneity.

I've chosen unschooling so that my children are part of life, not hidden away from it for thirteen years ~ the time commonly referred to as 'the best years of their lives'.

Unschooling begins from birth.
It's a way of life, and doesn't suddenly begin
at 4, 5, 6 or 7, as in formal, structured education.

Our children are always learning, and so are we.
Most of what we ever learn in life
we learn in our first few years anyway,
so it makes the idea of sending our children
off to someone else to learn
seem rather nonsensical.

Sharing Our Lives

Winter 2005/2006 ~ The Mother magazine, Issue 16

A few weeks ago, my family enjoyed six Bach suites played on solo cello at our independent bookshop, Bluebell. Afterwards, during supper, various people expressed surprise that there were children in attendance ~ you know, those creatures which should be seen, and not heard?

As I looked around the room, to my delight, I realised they were all unschoolers. This is because we don't separate our lives from 'education'. After all, why wouldn't children enjoy an early evening concert of deeply moving music? For many unschoolers, education is an expression of their Attachment Parenting lifestyle.

Our children's lives run alongside our own lives, sharing our interests as well as developing their own. Reading ranks as one of my favourite leisure activities, yet I rarely read fiction (as much as I love it, somehow it feels indulgent, and a voice inside me says that if I'm going to sit on my backside for hours, it needs to be 'educational').

My daughters have also developed this passion for reading. Eliza devours all things related to planets and animals. Bethany prefers her books to be fiction, and about love, love, love. We both share an appreciation of humour, so no doubt she'll enjoy the Bridget Jones diaries when she's older.

We were sent a fabulous vegan recipe for double choc chip muffins. The resident muffin makers got into action, and prepared a couple of trays to treat the family. I love this about unschooling ~ that we can do things when we want, and how we want.

The girls were at the museum in our nearest city, arranged by the local home education group. The theme was Diwali, and they were to make cards, and then partake (apparently!) in creating Indian music. The cards at the museum were already cut! And the colours and shapes had been dictated. The children were shown the picture they had to create. Everyone had to make a candle in the same colours, with the same shapes. I couldn't believe it. Is this the norm? Is this what happens in classroom/group activities? That children are meant to be creative according to what the teacher wants? It was a pointless exercise, and a waste of time and money. The children were bored. Interestingly (or not), the same thing happened in their French class. The French Christmas cards were made using stencils.

The children weren't even allowed to draw their own angel.

Back at the Indian music class, the facilitator let the children each have a brief turn at playing an instrument. I was speechless. What happened to the blurb which said they'd be 'creating music'? If this is education at its best, its most interesting, its most participative, then we seriously have to rethink the educational system our children are growing up in.

The UK government recently announced that it intends to bring in a curriculum for 0 – 3 year olds. Next they'll be dictating womb life! Why hasn't there been an overwhelming rejection of this by parents? Doesn't anyone care? Don't people see what's happening here? Our children aren't robots to be programmed.

Children need a childhood. They need to play, and yes, they need to be creative. This creativity comes from within them, and must never be dictated, or worse, eroded, by the teacher who has an expected outcome for a piece of work. So what, if a child draws an angel with black wings, or if a flower isn't pink or red? What's wrong with the *teachers* that they need to control every piece of art work so it can be an example of perfection as perceived by their own eyes?

At home, the girls can colour their flowers and angels any way they like. I can't help but wonder if my lack of artistic ability has anything to do with me not being allowed to express it freely in the classrooms of my childhood. It wouldn't surprise me. One heartless teacher stating that flowers aren't green, and that the petals are the wrong shape, would be enough to crush any child's inner flower.

The best of unschooling lies in the freedom to explore an unbounded imagination, not hampered by timetables, artificial learning environments, and prejudice.

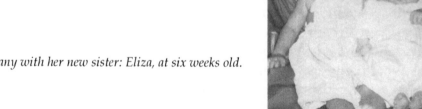

Bethany with her new sister: Eliza, at six weeks old.

The Cultural Soup

Most people who've been raised in modern society have been en-culturated by the erroneous belief that children need an education, and that it must happen in school, because teachers are experts at passing on 'education'. Even those of us who've removed ourselves from such a belief system are still caught in the cultural soup ~ an invisible energy ~ to some degree or another. We've been taught to believe that children learn in a structured environment, with an expert; and that learning happens in accordance with a specially de-signed, one-size-fits-all, curriculum.

As an unschooler, it soon becomes clear that learning is a unique experience, and that each family, and each child within that fam-ily, has their own way and style of learning. The main reason this book's not a manual is because no one family can tell another how to unschool. We may act as an example, but even if our way of life is truly inspiring, each family has its own dynamic, rhythm and way of living ~ and that always has to be honoured. It would be senseless to try and replicate that.

I recall meeting a well-established home educating family when my girls were toddlers, and feeling both overwhelmed and inspired when I entered their home. A girl was playing flute, teens were au-tonomously learning maths, a youngster was chopping up fruit, and Mum was making muffins, while Dad was planting vegetables in the polytunnel. So much activity! The house not only smelt fantastic, it felt alive and vibrant. What a wonderful environment in which to live and learn.

I was still at the point in my early parenting of not even having time to brush my hair, so the thought of actually 'educating' my children was for a time down the road. The template of that fam-ily's lifestyle, however, resonated strongly with me. The path ahead, if that's what home education looked like, seemed wonderful, but completely beyond my ability. The family's house was well-stocked with home education supplies ~ something mine never has been (for financial reasons). What I learnt, though, over the years, was that having fewer resources ended up making my girls *far more resource-ful* than if everything had been handed to them on a platter. Some home educating mothers and fathers are more accurately described as chauffeurs, because they spend so much time driving their children to activities. Even the thought of that exhausts me. While it's true that we do take our children out and about for things such as music lessons and stage writing classes, as often as possible the journey is combined with another activity, such as a chiropractic visit, or shopping at the organic fruit and vegetable market.

Bethany and Eliza helping gather organic fruit and vegetables at the local market. They've been learning about 'real life' in this way their whole lives.

Curiosity

Curiosity killed the cat
Satisfaction brought it back!

Curiosity is the key to a whole and balanced childhood ~ indeed, the key to a charmed life at any age.

As parents, if we offer a rich environment, the child will easily find what he needs in order to learn. We recognise that if a child desires to learn, then he'll enthusiastically absorb that information. This is the polar opposite of the rote learning and memorisation of subjects (compartmentalising information) which occurs in schools. Our culture severely underestimates the impact of imposing education upon children.

This quote from Napoleon Hill is very relevant to learning:

The starting point of all achievement is desire.
Keep this constantly in mind.
Weak desires bring weak results,
just as a small amount of fire makes a small amount of heat.

A zest for learning is not something you can force upon any human being, especially a child who naturally delights in life when left well alone. To truly understand something, you need to be irreverently in love with it, to have passion for it; otherwise, it's a fleeting relationship, the memory of which soon passes and disappears.

An unschooled child plays the lead role in the stage play of their life. Let's contrast this to school, where, in most cases, the teacher plays the lead, and is the instigator of activity. By allowing our children to immerse themselves in the lead role, they develop character, as Nature intended. They learn responsibility, inner discipline, independence. In school, the child is often cast as merely an 'extra'. They don't usually feel as if they're in charge of their life.

If you come into the home of an unschooling family, you won't find a pseudo classroom or timetables, any more than you'll see the parent playing school teacher. There are no lesson plans. No curriculum. No structure. That doesn't mean to say they don't use books or the Internet to inspire their learning. And it doesn't mean they don't have formal lessons for some topics, such as music.

So how do they learn? They do so from everyday living; from day-to-day experiences and activities; spontaneous conversations.

The primary element of this way of education is for the child to truly want to take part in their own learning.

As a parent, there's no greater teaching tool than to use your own life as an example. What are your life's passions? What gets you bouncing out of bed each day with enthusiasm? What is the lowest common denominator in your ethical charter? How do you relate to other people? How do you practise forgiveness and honesty? Are your children learning judgements about other people from your view?

When we, as parents, live life deliberately, consciously, ethically and with honesty, our children live and breathe our life performance. They're not excluded from our life, even if it seems at times they're on the periphery. They're not. They're Lead Character in their own life, and we, as parents, are on their periphery.

Our example of having hobbies or interests provides a starting place for children to develop theirs. Look at what sparks your child's imagination. If they love wildlife, allow them to explore this interest through drawing, books, a DVD, research, and most importantly of all, interacting with Nature. Give them the resources, space and time to create a wildlife garden. Old logs don't cost money. Every garden or nearby parkland can sneak in a small area in which to create a wildlife habitat. Let your child determine how much she wants to learn. Their passion doesn't need to be a thesis. If your child has had enough of a topic after five minutes, that's fine! And if she's there three months later, ready to lecture to your home education group about creating a wildlife garden, that's great, too. You see, both experiences are completely valid. One is not better than the other.

It's a far greater skill to ask questions than to know the answers to everything!

We don't learn about a field of information in one go. It happens bit by bit. This happens as an adult, too. Think about when you take on a new position of employment. No employer expects you to know the job back to front and inside out from day one. That would be ludicrous!

When we unschool, we're generous with our children, and let them gather the information they need, over time.

Houses are built brick by brick, after putting down a foundation. We don't put on the roof if the walls or posts and beams aren't up. And learning is no different.

It's too easy to overlook just how much our children are learning, especially if it seems they sit around drawing or reading fiction all day. Somehow we expect to see the house built. We're culturally conditioned to tick boxes. We want to measure their growth. We want a yardstick of what's gone into their brain. And, in our obsession with this, we really don't appreciate that while they were making chocolate cake or playing dress-ups, our kids were at the back of the house building the verandah! We missed it because we were focused on the roof! And can you see, this is *our* problem, our agenda; not theirs? Even at home, away from the mainstream institution of schooling, we're still slaves to the process of trying to define education.

In a traditional education system, children are monitored every step of the way to see if they're 'learning'. Now, I use the word learning loosely, in this case, because more often than not, learning isn't what's happening. It's down to *memorising*. When we can finally let go of all methods of measuring so-called progress, this frees our children up enormously to learn in a whole way.

As a parent of unschooled children, I've recognised how crucial it is to be curious about the life around us; and if we can focus on exploring our own interests, we'll witness this become a diving board for the children to navigate their own learning path.

Bare-bottomed Bethany being very curious about what was in her Dad's toiletry bag.

Eliza enjoying the Spring sunshine.
Below: Bethany and Veronika say hello to a wandering cat, New Zealand.

Learning From Real Life

Our children aren't isolated from the real world, they're part of it. They're not separated from friends by age, and they're not separated from family. They are an active part of our local community. As parents, we don't sanitise their lives by hiding real life issues, such as illness, age, financial situations. We embrace, rather than hide, the experiences of life. And this is a fundamental aspect of this approach to education: children learn from life by being part of it. There have been aspects of our life that have been incredibly difficult. We didn't hide them from our children.

In 2003, when the girls were aged seven and five, we bought a small piece of land, of about four acres, which we called Earthsong. The dream was to plant an organic orchard, and lead a self-sufficient lifestyle. What we didn't know was that the dream would turn into a nightmare: a legal nightmare.

As a family, we planted hundreds of fruit trees (many varieties of apple, pear and plum) into deep trenches one icy cold February day. We created an orchard ~ a gift to Earth that would last many, many years, and offer Nature benefits that would be invisible to our eyes. There were many other jobs that we did on the land ~ building a stable, erecting a polytunnel, putting up fences, rotovating the ground, as well as growing herbs, vegetables, flowers and berries. All of these were a labour of love. I can't even begin to put a value on how much my girls were enriched by having this piece of land as part of their early childhood. Their days were fun, rich, joyous and adventurous. Every single moment on our smallholding was a spectacular learning adventure for all of us. I'm so thankful for this, as it helped to provide some cushioning to what was to become one of the most difficult times of our lives.

Our piece of land came with a 'right of way', which meant we had to travel across someone else's field to get there. Our deeds came with a map which showed us we should travel in a straight line from the main road, across the farmer's field, and to our entry gate. To cut a painful, long story short, the farmer ignored our deed, and took us to court on the grounds we were 'trespassing' because we wouldn't drive in his deep tractor ruts on a camber (which was impossible in our car), rather than straight across the field ~ despite this having been the access for previous farmers for well over 100 years. Ironically, the deed was drawn up in the first place by the firm of solicitors representing the farmer! They declared the deed (which they had drawn up) was irrelevant. Talk about a conflict of interest!

The children were witness to their parents' deep stress ~ emotional and financial. Bethany and Eliza also witnessed first hand that the legal system doesn't always lead to justice being served. They saw how the local farmers lied to avoid being bullied by 'one of their own', even if that was a person they detested. Ironically, some time later, the Crown Prosecution Service took the farmer in question to court without our knowledge ~ and prosecuted him ~ for attacking me and the girls one day as we were leaving the land. In that case, the girls saw legal justice, even if we didn't feel like winners.

As a result of the 'right of way' court case, we were left in no other position but to declare ourselves bankrupt. Our progress through these times, as well as all of our years living on a budget which offers little leeway for luxuries, has taught them far more about finance than any school subject could. And ironically, through it all, they've learnt what abundance really means, and that is that real wealth is what you have left when all the money is gone. The girls are also learning that even, and especially, in difficult times like that, forgiveness is the greatest healer. This isn't taught in schools. Our culture is based on blame and shame, and it's in the interest of our culture to sustain this belief.

When Paul's mother had her flu vaccine in December, 2006, and became ill from it, we assumed that she'd be better by Christmas. Each year we'd travel over to South Shields, and share Christmas day with her in her tiny flat. That year, she was in and out of hospital. We did many trips to visit her. On Christmas day we sat by her bed. Within a few weeks she was dead.

On the day she died, the girls were with us, and held her hand, cuddled her, and told her how much they loved her. They were witnesses to a very natural part of life that most people never experience. If they'd been in school, it would have been difficult, if not impossible, for them to visit her so regularly in those last weeks.

Unlike many home educators, we don't spend a lot of time going from museum to museum. We've enjoyed museums and art galleries, but they've not been a staple of our education, but delectable treats to be savoured.

Instead, the girls have taken part in other aspects of community, such as attending the local knitting café with women of all ages, and attending summer camps run by an outdoor community group (Eden Community Outdoors). There, they participated in abseiling, canoeing, wood turning, drama. When they were younger, they attended the Eden Valley Storytellers. They've also helped me to run camps for The Mother magazine, and so have been part of the process of building a temporary community from scratch. Events like this are always a steep learning curve, because when you bring together so many people, with various needs, as an organiser you're effectively trying to achieve the impossible. And that's without even factoring in the potential for awful weather!

In 2008, the girls took a petition to number ten Downing Street to speak up about the lack of government support for, and ostracising of, breastfeeding families. This is citizenship education in action. They've learnt that although we live in a democratic country it can be very hard for the person on the street to speak up.

Taking a petition to Downing Street.

Jump off! Bethany playing on a mound of dirt at the edge of our village.

"Mum, I'm bored!"

"Boredom is unearned leisure."
Author unknown

Boredom can happen to any child; it isn't the domain of unschooled children. In fact, you'll find that the children who suffer most from boredom are school children on holidays, and children with structured lives. You can hear this echoed back in the voices of many harried mothers who say "I can't wait till they're back in school!" How very sad.

When faced with large expanses of time, school children often don't know what to do. This rarely happens for an unschooled child, as there are always plenty of projects on the go, or ideas to pursue. Their lives are interesting, as they've learnt to be self-motivated. If you've recently taken your child out of school, you might find this chapter particularly relevant.

It stimulates our own growth as parents when we cease to dismiss boredom as equally as we avoid trying to fix it. If your child wasn't feeling great, you'd honour and acknowledge that. Well, it's the same with boredom. It doesn't mean there's something wrong with your child, or that she's lazy. Children need to trust their parents. We really ought not to belittle or punish bored children by giving them housework ~ tempting though it might be to have a bit of free child labour!

Our role is to provide guidance and empathy ~ to imagine being their age (perhaps in ongoing extreme weather conditions [blizzards or gales], in a particular environment). We ask ourselves how we'd move forward in difficult circumstances. Are they bored because they're unhappy? Sad? Sometimes children just need a change of scene: to go for a walk, to have an adventure; to eat something; to be cuddled.

Recognise that boredom often comes in disguise, regardless of the child's age. We might see it as whining, irritability, tiredness, not wanting to 'think'. If we're aware, we might recognise that the child is in need of some one-on-one parent time. Maybe sleep is needed, regardless of the time of day. Often, the underlying issue is a need for change. As a parent, we, too, learn many things when crossing the great boredom divide. We learn compassion, awareness and creativity when we turn our own boredom into adventure. If all else fails, I find that no matter what the age: just add water! Watering the garden; a hot bath; spa; swimming; taking a walk on the beach, by the river; washing the dishes in warm, soapy water. Water has amazing capacities for changing the energetic space a person is in.

A few years back, when both girls were able to fit in the bathtub at the same time, there was a rather loud commotion coming from our bathroom. When I went to investigate, I found the girls having a fabulous time. Eliza was scooping up little bubbles from the shampoo, putting them into a small container, and doing Bubble Reading. Bubble Reading was her version of Tea Leaf Reading. Bethany was beside herself with hysterics when Eliza predicted that her older sister would marry Johnny Depp.

The Bubble Girls, Christmas 1998.

A Time To Play

"All of the animals except for man
know that the principal business of life is to enjoy it."
~ Samuel Butler

Mother Nature ordained that childhood was a time exclusively for play. How do we know this? We see lambs frolicking in the field, and young foals prancing with delight. Kittens and lion cubs rough and tumble for hours on end.

Human babies do aqua aerobics in the womb. After birth, our breastfed babes play with their mothers' nipples. Babies play peek-a-boo with their mothers' faces. And yet, our culture is increasingly enforcing lifestyles and education systems which take away opportunities for natural play, replacing them with adult agendas and adult-supervised or controlled 'play'.

Play is often thought of as something for little kids, as if it has no value in real life. The UK government introduced 'controlled play', where adults determine what the children are learning, and how they're playing. Imagine that, an adult telling a child how to play! It's a symptom of our cultural blindness.

Play has lost its place in our society, and yet it's vital to learning. The beauty of unschooling is that it allows the whole family to play. Adults need to play, as much as children. What does play generate? Happiness. Joy. Fun. Satisfaction. Our society, in general, doesn't place enough value on the importance of free play, and tends to relegate it to outside of school time. If we look to the goal of school, we see that it has one purpose: to get students ready for the job market so they'll be of benefit to society. Kids are on a production line. There simply isn't the room for something as unproductive as fun! But what's the point of life if we don't enjoy it?

I believe one of the things we really become clearer about when unschooling is the true meaning of life and life values. We simply don't tolerate the sheep mentality (sheeple) and the automatic authoritarian attitude that is often forced upon us. As parents and as adults, unschooling as a way of life is growth: an evolution. Without noticing it creep up on us, we become very confident in ourselves as human beings and deliberate creators of our life.

One of the hardest aspects of adapting to unschooling, as something different from the norm, is recognising that we, as adults, need to completely let go of everything we've ever been told about education. It doesn't serve the road we're travelling on. *The school model of education is completely irrelevant to the unschooling family.* It's not just our beliefs about school/education which need to be ditched, it's also our compulsion for comparison. It's an addiction. There's not one other child on this whole planet to whom you should compare your child. Ever! And that really is a hard thing to let go of for many parents as they seek to define their way through uncharted territory. Mainstream education is based upon this principle. It's called grades. It's called testing. It's called competition. In fact, we do this to babies in utero with scanning. Before our children are even born, we're comparing their head and body length measurements to *other* babies. This continues after birth, with weights and heights and percentiles. When you wake up to what's happening, you really see how our culture is addicted to it, and sets us up for constant measuring. One of the first questions we're asked after birth is "how much did your baby weigh?" And then, from the moment we're born, someone is trying to change us. Why? Because we've been compared to someone else ~ and someone has decided that we don't measure up. Where's the love in that? As an unschooling mother, I don't compare my children's progress to other children. They're completely free to learn in their own way and time. They also choose what to learn.

"Play as a state requires,
first and foremost,
that you be safe.
You can't be safe if somebody's there
measuring and censoring, judging,
evaluating."
~ Michael Mendizza

The Toy Box

*"We don't stop playing because we grow old,
we grow old because we stop playing."*
~ George Bernard Shaw

The children's toy box provided a place to find props for play, whether they were hand-made dolls, dressing up clothes, wooden blocks or wooden toys ~ like a horse's cart. The characters the girls made were from fabric, card, paper, grass and sticks. They also had a collection of fabric dolls and animals crocheted by my mother, and some from a Single Mothers' Cooperative in Brazil.

I found the old, dusty chest at an auction, and bought it for just a couple of pounds. We painted the latticed sides white. The fabric lid makes a seat for children's bottoms, or for toys to parade upon.

For the past ten years, this space has been home to various toys, fabrics and an accumulation of Nature collections!

When I reflect on the toys that my children played with, I see how clearly Nature was part of their playtime: mud, flowers, wooden blocks with bark, sticks, pine cones, pebbles, berries, branches, feathers, clouds and hedges. We've enjoyed long walks each day through all the seasons of the year.

Hand-made toys were complemented by dressing up in old bits of fabric, or concocting potions from herbs and flowers in the garden, and putting them into small glass jars; or creating paper, grass or fabric dolls. Their childhood was defined by an absence of plastic toys and television, and this meant that their imagination was able to express itself fully through play.

Many modern children are prescribed medication to calm their excess energy ~ and suppress their souls ~ to keep them sitting in a school seat for several hours a day. Unschooled children who have the time, space and freedom to play as they desire, are able to live out their energy as Nature planned. Children need trees to climb; woods to explore; naturally lying or flowing water to investigate; to feel the wind on their cheeks, and the Sun on their shoulders; moonlight on their eyelashes. Soil needs to get under the fingers, and seeds must collect in their hair. These are the badges of a free range childhood.

I'll never regret that my children's childhood was based entirely on play. How could I? Whether it was making mud cakes down at the old chicken house under the pine trees, dressing up as white witches or queens, collecting berries for crumble, or cutting up fabric, card and paper to make dolls, their imaginations were enlivened.

As unschooled children, their afternoons aren't bogged down by homework. There aren't demands for good grades, or expectations in relation to what they're learning. Afternoons, like the rest of the time, are dedicated to playing, exploring and being with the family.

During play, there's much happening in the mind and heart of a child. These 'non-conscious processes' are integral to how easily and happily a child learns. Given that the most learning ~ and the greatest learning we ever do ~ happens within the *first 36 months of life*, when the child is not even *aware* of learning, there's clearly much we have, as adults, to discover about how learning works.

Learning happens in so many ways, and it would be naïve to think education was based on lessons put into neat categories like maths; literacy; science; geography; and history. As a family, our intimate community of four provides daily lessons in living. From each other we learn about kindness, forgiveness, empathy, compassion, anger, patience and awareness. Because we love each other deeply, we have a safe space to explore our shadows, as well as the areas where we shine.

Unschooling has a different energy compared to that of the average classroom. Shame and blame are not the goalposts which define the narrow entry point to success: love, respect and nurturing are. Choosing which toys to play with, and how to play, are where unschooled children get a sense of feeling in charge of their own decision making.

Eliza's almost 12, and it's only been in the past six or so months that she's really stopped playing with her dolls, though she quite happily still plays dolls with a five year old girl up the road. And she was ever so delighted when a parcel came from her grandmother in Australia the other day ~ it contained a selection of miniature dolls' clothes.

I never was much of a doll girl when I was a child ~ I was pure tomboy! Outside: climbing trees; racing go karts; playing in the creek; making empires with my Matchbox cars in the dirt ~ pretty dolls had no real place in my childhood, for some reason. It's been fascinating for me to watch Eliza and Bethany play with dolls so intensely and contentedly for years on end. I've marvelled at the plots, storylines, characters and resolutions.

Their 'toy box' now, as adolescents, has inevitably changed over the years, and includes, amongst other things: musical instruments, easels, paintbrushes and pens, board games, knitting needles, sewing baskets and books. They write, read, read, read, and sing and play music. Nature is one of their greatest resources, and never more so than in Summer ~ a time for foraging, and disappearing out of the village, away from the eyes of adults.

The Toy Box, by Bethany

Their childhood was defined by an absence of plastic toys and television, and this meant that their imagination was able to express itself fully through play.

Eliza's learnt that she can avoid my influence
quite easily these days,
particularly if there's the remotest suggestion
that she might like to tidy her bedroom.
In two seconds she can be on her bike,
and up the village, out of sight.

Eliza and Bethany under the plum trees.

Bullies on the Village Green

Summer, 2005 ~ The Mother magazine, Issue 14

My girls are growing up. Not only do I see it in the way they're shooting up like bean sprouts (of the Jack and the Beanstalk variety), but also by noticing how my influence on them is rapidly diminishing. Each week someone new seems to come along who acts as a role model in some way. The gorgeous women at the knitting café have, beautifully, taken my girls under their wings, teaching them to knit, crochet, make pompoms and tassels. Our neighbour, Rose, showed Bethany how to knit her first hat. She's also given her a collection of wool. Rose used to own a wool shop in London many years ago. No wonder Bethany thinks of her as a Fairy Godmother.

From another person, Bethany's been learning the ancient art of scything. She loves it. There's something rather Zen-like about the movements which are required to do it effectively and gracefully.

During the girls' weekly French group, I go for a walk or catch up on some work. One hour on my own isn't to be taken lightly. At the end of term, the parents were invited to see what the children had been learning. I had my first taste of how Eliza and Bethany fit into a formal learning environment. Needless to say they were the only children who spoke when they felt inspired, rather than when they were 'allowed' to speak. They didn't put their hands up to speak, and they didn't sit up nicely like all the other children. Oh no, not my kids. They lay all over the floor, legs wide apart ~ me thinking "Oh Goddess, I hope Eliza's got knickers on today." Fortunately, she had.

Eliza's learnt that she can avoid my influence quite easily these days, particularly if there's the remotest suggestion that she might like to tidy her bedroom. In two seconds she can be on her bike, and up the village, out of sight. You wouldn't believe how quickly a seven year old can scramble out of the back door. The monkey! High time I installed a webcam on the village green. Or perhaps I need to attach electronic tags to their wee ankles.

They say it takes a whole village to raise a child. Well, having seen the village lately, I'll raise my kids myself, thank you very much!

There have been many nights when the girls have cried themselves to sleep as they deal with rejections, and oftentimes nastiness, from some of the children in the village. It's been breaking my heart.

Paul and I spend the longest time talking with the girls about positive ways to get through this. Our suggestions seem in vain. For the first time in six years, I feel ready to pack our bags and move. And yet I know that moving elsewhere isn't the answer. At some point, my children will meet other children who, too, will delight in using them as a cheap source of entertainment. We're looking for the positives in the situation, and showing our children how to remain strong, while honouring their hurt feelings, and not to feel victimised.

We're affirming that all the wonderful things we love about them are still true and valid, and worth celebrating; that they have their own free-thinking minds; that they're special and caring because they make home-made gifts, and take joy in such simple pleasures; and their imaginations are alive and brilliant. It isn't easy, but we're getting there. One of my initial reasons for home education was to avoid school bullies. How ironic to have them on the village green. I knew our alternative lifestyle would make the girls prime candidates for this. It's common thinking that 'children are cruel, and it's part of life'. But where do these children learn to be cruel? I don't believe we're born with an inbuilt sense of wanting to torment another human being. This isn't the true nature of any human being. It's learned behaviour. Who taught these children not to celebrate diversity, but to discriminate?

It's common thinking that
'children are cruel, and it's part of life'.

But where do these children
learn to be cruel?

I don't believe we're born with an inbuilt sense
of wanting to
torment another human being.
This isn't the true nature of any human being.
It's learned behaviour.

Intentional Solitude

All children need time alone, regardless of whether they're five or fifteen, in school or not.

Silence is refreshing to the soul. As humans, we need time to go inwards, to reflect, and to nurture our inner world ~ through daydreams, rest, and quiet contemplation. This is where we create our world.

Solitude is increasingly rare for modern children, whose days are filled with organised activity, followed by hours and hours of televisual stimulus, and company.

In school, the teachers were forever yelling at me to 'stop daydreaming', and their roar would haul me back in from the clouds upon whose soft, fluffy backs I was lazing. It seems ironic that those 'experts' on children were completely unaware that the very thing a child needs IS to daydream! It's more vital to education than reading, writing and 'rithmetic!

When we're in this place of 'soft time', our brain has the chance to integrate everything we've been absorbing. It makes sense of all the material that has come into the conscious and subconscious. And it does this without us telling it how.

I've come to believe that telling children not to daydream is tantamount to child abuse.

It isn't unusual
to see her lying gracefully on her bed,
quiet and still.

"Shhhhh" she whispers, "I'm being
Sleeping Beauty."

No Lessons Today
Winter, 2002 ~ The Mother magazine, Issue 4

It's 6am, and Bethany asks with an excitement I can't quite reconcile with this time of the morning, or with mathematics: "Do you want to hear the nine times tables?" "Er, no…" I mutter quietly, as I try and slip back into my dream state, pillow over my head just in case the request comes again. "I'll listen," her Dad says. That's why I love him so much. He lets me sleep!

Never did I imagine the times tables being so popular. It happened by accident, really. I was browsing in the school textbook section of our brilliant independent bookshop, Bluebell, when I came across a Ladybird book/cassette with times tables. Each is sung to a different tune by a different person. They're really catchy! I must confess that Bethany now knows more times tables than I do. My memory is of thirty kids repeating them out loud in the most deadpan voices ever. Now I find myself singing them even without the cassette on, or children in earshot.

I've noticed four year old Eliza picking up quite a few as well. She'd have to, really, it's become Bethany's accessory: got cassette, must play it in the car.

I came downstairs this morning to find Bethany writing out all the times tables she knows ~ without the book or cassette to prompt her. I told her that one of the great things about unschooling is that kids learn to just get on and do things, and they don't need Mum or Dad to organise lessons or activities for them all the time. She was quite impressed by this.

Play. That's where it's really at. They play Steiner Schools ~ which means that it's Bethany's excuse to be bossy by pretending she's a teacher, and lining up all the toys and Eliza, while she chooses which songs they'll sing, and stories they'll act out.

Eliza's idea of fun is to use the envelopes that new subscriptions come in to 'write cheques' for various things. She's busy budgeting in her games.

I'm not a mum who has the week mapped out with lots of outings and visits to friends. I prefer the sanctuary of my own space, and I feel the children do, too. Sure we go out and do things, but there's always a sense of "Ah, we're home again!"

Last Winter, my mother sent us the novel, *The Secret Garden*. I could never have imagined how this would impact on our day-to-day life. It started all rather gently and beautifully, really. We'd sit snuggled up together by the fire each evening as Paul read a chapter out in his best Yorkshire accent. We all really looked forward to it. And then there was that feeling you get at the end of any good book: satisfaction, but a certain sadness that it's over. Well, it wasn't over for Bethany. She soon got a Ladybird first reader version of The *Secret Garden*. Needless to say she knows it scene by scene.

The first time it happened, I nearly broke both my legs running up the stairs to find out what was going on. A blood curdling scream had erupted out of nowhere, in the bedroom. Who'd killed who? I arrived breathless. "What's wrong?" I asked, amazed to see no murderer in the room, and both girls sitting calmly on the bed. "Nothing's wrong," Bethany answered, surprised by my arrival. "I'm just being Colin from *The Secret Garden*, having a tantrum." This scene has now taken place hundreds of times. I'm not exaggerating. She really loves it. So, between them, Bethany and Eliza play all the scenes. They spend hours at this, which will answer the frequently asked question: "How do you get time to edit The Mother magazine?" Simple. My kids play!

The downside of this, and yes, there is one, is that after several scenes, just about every item of clothing they own has been worn and tossed aside! Life is a constant dress rehearsal for them, and a constant re-sorting of clothes for me.

A year ago, I was banned from reading any fairy tales. The thought of someone or something nasty in a story was too much for Bethany. All that's changed now that she's discovered that they all live happily ever after. It isn't unusual to see her lying gracefully on her bed, quiet and still. "Shhhhh" she whispers, "I'm being Sleeping Beauty."

Then along came Snow White. This new character is directly responsible for the apple consumption in our home increasing by two kilograms a week ~ and that's just for the dress rehearsals between her and the wicked witch.

Success and Failure

To let go of false ideas about education means recognising that your child can never ever fail, and nor can you. Let me repeat this: you can not fail at unschooling. By not comparing your child to others, and by being receptive to their spontaneous learning, what you might find is that they have the capacity to introduce *you* to new ideas every day. All we need to do, as parents, is to provide as much of life as we can.

By bringing the world into our homes, with joy and enthusiasm, it's inevitable that our children will ask questions. It's human nature. We just have to stand back, and to trust. Our children are born curious. When we unschool, they integrate all that's learnt in our day-to-day living. They're immersed in their chosen passions. They challenge themselves as much as they desire. In many ways, this is the finest inner discipline we can acquire. Trust is a requirement of the decision to unschool. This means trusting our children, and trusting ourselves, that we're on the right path: trusting ourselves, in spite of what the cultural messages are.

Many years ago, I was rather unhappy in a job. I worked as a laboratory assistant in the local hospital's medical laboratory (quite funny, in hindsight, given I'd failed science all the way through school!), and was being sexually harassed by the laboratory manager.

The hospital counsellor spoke with me, and asked what job I'd like to do if I could wave a wand. "I'd love to write for a newspaper!" I told her very enthusiastically, my eyes lighting up for the first time in months. She then asked the rather obvious question: "Have you been to see the editor of the local newspaper?" "Erm, no." It hadn't even occurred to me that I could possibly work on a newspaper without having done a degree.

Well, I plucked up the courage, and phoned him. He invited me down for a chat. He had no job to offer me, but asked if I was willing to come down each day after my laboratory job, and work voluntarily for an hour or so doing the emergency rounds. This involved phoning the ambulance, fire and police to see if they had any stories. I jumped at this opportunity.

I loved the buzz of being in the newsroom. Ironically, all the trouble I got into at school for looking at my keyboard during typing lessons seemed a joke, because I no longer had the time to look at it. I just had to type! In school, the teacher would hit my knuckles with a ruler whenever she caught me looking at the keyboard. Then she placed a large 'bib' over my hands and arms, hoping humiliation and shame would do the trick! Not surprisingly, I ended up dropping typing as a subject. Looking back, I can't believe such 'teaching' methods were allowed! No small wonder I hated school.

And so I learnt to touch type. By the end of the first week, on the Friday evening, the editor came in and said to me, "We've got no reporters to cover for the weekend. Will you do it?" You can imagine: every emotion from A-Z. I was so thrilled, and more than a little freaked out. Back then, on local papers, reporting also included photography. The editor took me over to one of the cameras, showed me how to load some film, and said, "See you on Monday." My obvious reward was a front page article, and the permission to start writing features: but it was so much more than that. I'd had my fire lit. You might wonder what relevance this has to a book on unschooling. Well, it has everything to do with it, actually. This man completely trusted me to 'learn' the trade without any interference from him or journalists on the newspaper. In school, we're told what to do. We're rewarded and punished. As soon as we introduce fear, confusion or even boredom into the learning arena, we limit the ability to absorb information. A lot of learning happens without us even being aware of it. It's called spontaneous learning.

Unschooling is holistic total education at its finest. It involves our whole being, including feelings. When we feel safe, we learn more easily. When we feel scared, the path becomes blocked in our brain. The pressure to sit tests, and the feeling we're being judged, are not conducive to good learning. Learning, by its nature, is meant to be enjoyable. Your child is unique. When she's ready to learn something, she will. There's no need to 'teach' her. The fire of interest has to be internal.

Some years ago, I worked as a Media Officer for the RSPCA, in New Zealand. One of the tasks was to write a book on the history of animal welfare in that country. That was the easy part. I felt strongly about designing the book, and doing the layout myself; just one small, teeny-tiny problem. I'd never used a design package before. I kept asking the secretary in the office to help me because I always seemed to lock up the computer. One day she really lost her fuse, and screamed at me, "I've never seen anyone so computer illiterate!" OUCH! I still hear her venomous tone in my ears. I managed to get the book together, and was rather chuffed. Roll forward about 14 years to when I decided to start a magazine, and the same scenario presented itself. I couldn't locate the design programme I'd used all those years ago, with which I was slightly familiar ~ so I was going to have to start from scratch. How on Earth was I going to lay out the magazine? But you know, in my own safe environment, with a desire to learn, I managed to do it. It took a bit of trial and error, I might add, not to mention a bunch of swear words; but there was no-one on my case yelling at me or putting me under pressure to perform. No one, that is, except myself. To be honest, I cringe when I look at the layout of the early issues of The Mother magazine, but I'm also pleased that I've managed to learn two design programmes without a single text book, or voice booming down my ear about how stupid I am, even if it did take a number of years! Technology isn't my forté.

As parents, the more we can back off from our children's learning experiences, the better off they'll be. We can provide resources, make suggestions, and help find tricky answers. We can even find someone to give lessons ~ for example, piano ~ or let them join a group of interest (wildlife, language or drama). The key to any successful learning experience is that it's relaxed and pleasurable. And just as we might find others to offer guidance in areas we're not familiar with, likewise we can offer insights to other people's children in our chosen areas. LETS, The Local Exchange Trade System, is a green approach to bartering, where you swap services with people, rather than money. The same can be applied to unschooling/home education. What skills, talents, hobbies or interests do you have that can benefit other people's children? Likewise, you can find people for your children to apprentice with. This can begin at any age where they express an interest in a topic. I'm lousy at art. And yet, instead of feeling inadequate when I see how skilled my daughters are with drawing compared to me, I can ask a great friend who's an artist, to 'guide' them. She'll quite happily sit with the girls without 'teaching' them to draw ~ just offering tips and encouragement.

We learn from random things all the time. Our curiosity gets sparked in numerous ways. When we're travelling, a conversation about something pretty basic leads to all sorts of questions, and then answers. Or something we see on our journey, like a black horse, or a truck with funny words written on it, sets off another conversation. Curiosity builds upon itself. Once the flame is ignited, the interest increases, then there's a big fire. This is learning! Believe me, it really is that simple.

The interest always has to come before learning if we expect any value from the experience. It's vital we step outside the box when approaching different learning situations. I used to mentally clock how many subjects we were covering when doing any particular activity. For example, if we were cooking, I'd be thinking, oh great, we're doing maths because we're measuring, counting, weighing. And then there's the chemistry which happens between the ingredients. Let's not forget the geography when discussing the origin of the ingredients. We'd discuss environmental implications, agriculture and so on. I've let go of that. We simply don't need to keep score. It's another form of measuring, and it really is unnecessary. Natural learning is organic, and covers so many areas, that it inevitably makes any school timetable or curriculum look rather lame.

Life's a broad, vast and rich canvas, and it's upon this that the unschooling family weaves and draws its own threads. By allowing children the freedom to express, learning can come in so many ways.

A rather conservative friend once pointed out to me that my children stood out whenever we were in town: that you could tell they were home-educated; she said, "you know, they dress a little differently!"

At eight, Eliza desperately wanted to wear one of those rather hideous Disney fairytale princess dresses someone had given her. Her older sister, Bethany, who was ten at the time, had recently had a kick of pubescent hormones (which I can tell you, was a whole life education for all of us!); and she was horrified at the thought of her sister wearing THAT dress to town. Two months previous to that, she wouldn't have thought twice. She'd have worn it herself.

By allowing Eliza to wear her ball-length gown to town, we all let go of whatever issues we might have had surrounding that. One day, she'd had enough of her hair style, and wanted to wear a long scarf on her head, to town. Again, her sister reacted and said, "People will think she's Muslim." (Just for clarity, we've no prejudice against Muslims, it was Bethany being concerned about mis-identity). Eliza's reaction was that she didn't care what anyone thought about her! Even now, she still has the same attitude. I find it rather admirable, particularly because most children have already learnt to conform by this age. It was, to me, simply another example of what learning and education include.

Learning goes way beyond maths, literacy and the sciences. Our schools, sadly, have education pinned down to a handful of subjects, with maths and literacy taking prime place. Unfortunately, many people enter home education with the notion that they have to place these two subjects at the head of the learning queue, regardless of whether the 'flame' of interest is there for the child.

It's vital we step outside the box when approaching different learning situations.

Eliza and Bethany having a race on the land we owned.

Without praise, we shrivel.
Without praise, we flounder.

Without praise,
we have no external signposts
to help us find our own self-acceptance.

Cattle Branding
Searing the soul with grades, tests and certificates

"Grades aren't everything. It's the learning that counts.
Even eggs get graded!"
Laura Ingalls to Nellie Olsen, Little House on the Prairie.

I grew up on the Darling Downs, which is predominantly beef raising land. Cattle were branded, that is, their hide was burnt into with a hot iron, to identify which farmer owned them. There have been many times I've wondered how far into the skin our branding of children goes, and just who owns them and their learning.

When Eliza was in school, she brought home a certificate proclaiming her to be 'talented in writing'. As a mother, I didn't need a certificate or report cards to tell me what I already knew. I'd seen the novels she'd been working on, as well as her poems.

The certificate was from an organisation which asks school children to write a short paragraph on a particular topic. It then sends the certificates out, stating they have this particular talent, and a letter to the parents saying their child's writing is so good it's going to be published! So good, in fact, and so publishable, that the parents themselves are paying for the publication!

Vanity publishing is the oldest trick in the book, because there are few people who don't want to see their name, or their child's name, in print. Even when you can see through the lies and scam, it's still an awfully difficult position, as a parent, to be in: telling your child that you aren't going to 'pay for them' to be in the book could be taken as a sign by the child that you don't think their writing's any good.

We explained to Eliza about such schemes, and that we knew she was a very good writer. We also know she'd love to be a published fiction writer, and so we've encouraged her to write her own books (which she's doing). This way, she sees the process involved, and that it's actually a lot different to a parent paying for a book to be published which contains *one* paragraph of their writing.

Issuing children stickers, stamps, certificates or report cards is a measuring stick of one moment in time. It doesn't illuminate their soul in the way that their own observations of growth do. Grades are a 'marker', a form of branding, and they don't have the potential to liberate genius and brilliance (which all children possess) in the same way that honest self-direction does.

Bethany's chosen to undertake music exams for piano and violin. At no point have Paul and I ever insisted she takes them, however her music teacher is very exam focused. If we'd been aware at the start, we'd have perhaps chosen a different teacher. Regardless, Bethany has a good rapport with her, and that's something to take into consideration.

Bethany's learning the hard way, though, that exams are not always an accurate reflection of a student's ability; and that nerves, performance anxiety, hormonal dips, not to mention the examiner's mood, perception, and ability to remember what's on the child's syllabus (so they don't terrify the student by asking for something a grade or two above them), all have a role to play in the final result. An exam result doesn't take into account that the day before, a student had played a piece 'perfectly'.

Playing music for pleasure is the key, and if Bethany feels that having certificates will help her later on in life, then that's her choice. She's considering her options, such as changing teacher, or perhaps not doing exams until grade eight.

Eliza, on the other hand, who was quite keen to do exams for saxophone, has gone from grade 1 to grade 3 overnight, and given her maverick, 'don't-label-me' personality, isn't as inclined to take exams to prove she's good enough. Her pleasure comes not from grades, but from knowing she can play a certain level piece that a day or a week ago seemed impossibly hard. The feeling of success will give more meaning to her, not to mention more incentive, than any piece of paper ~ even one with distinction embossed in gold. Having said that, she's quite keen to 'try' an exam ~ for the experience ~ and is preparing for grade three, as well as entering a music festival in Carlisle city. In her favour is that she doesn't have a nervous disposition ~ one of the biggest downfalls in musical exams.

Sacred Praise

There's something rather poisonous slipping into modern parenting dogma, and it's that of *not* praising children. The belief is that if you praise your child s/he will only do things to get more praise. Personally, I think this is rubbish. I've spent much time exploring the idea, and came back to my intuitive feel, which is that praise is sacred. Praise is the cousin of gratitude, which is the most important feeling we can ever have in the world.

I believe we all need to be praised, valued, held up, nourished into fullness, and adored. I believe that those who advocate not praising our children are people who've perhaps not felt the benefits of ample praise themselves.

I do caution against praise for praise's sake! There's nothing more stomach-turning to me than insincere praise. Children know when we're insincere anyway, so there's no point lying or pretending something's great. Be honest. Be radically honest, and be kind. The key, I feel, is for praise to be in the present moment, not used as a carrot for future work or achievements.

Praise is like sunshine on your shoulders, water on a growing flower, moonlight rising above a mountain on a dark night, your favourite meal cooked with love, like the arms of your mother around you when you've scraped your knee. Praise lifts you. It raises you to be all you can be. Praise acknowledges and witnesses your journey through life. Praise teaches us about self care, and helps us to see what others see in us.

Without praise, we shrivel. Without praise, we flounder. Without praise, we have no external signposts to help us discover our self-acceptance.

Religions around the world praise God, and God by any other name. We praise Him/Her/All that is, and yet the children made in His image are not considered worthy of praise because some parenting guru says so? Listen to your heart. Imagine how you feel when you produce work, projects, or do little acts of change as gifts to this world ~ and no one acknowledges your place within it. Children are constantly gifting this world with their miracles. Let's not have them believing their place isn't important just because the latest fad is to withhold genuine acknowledgement.

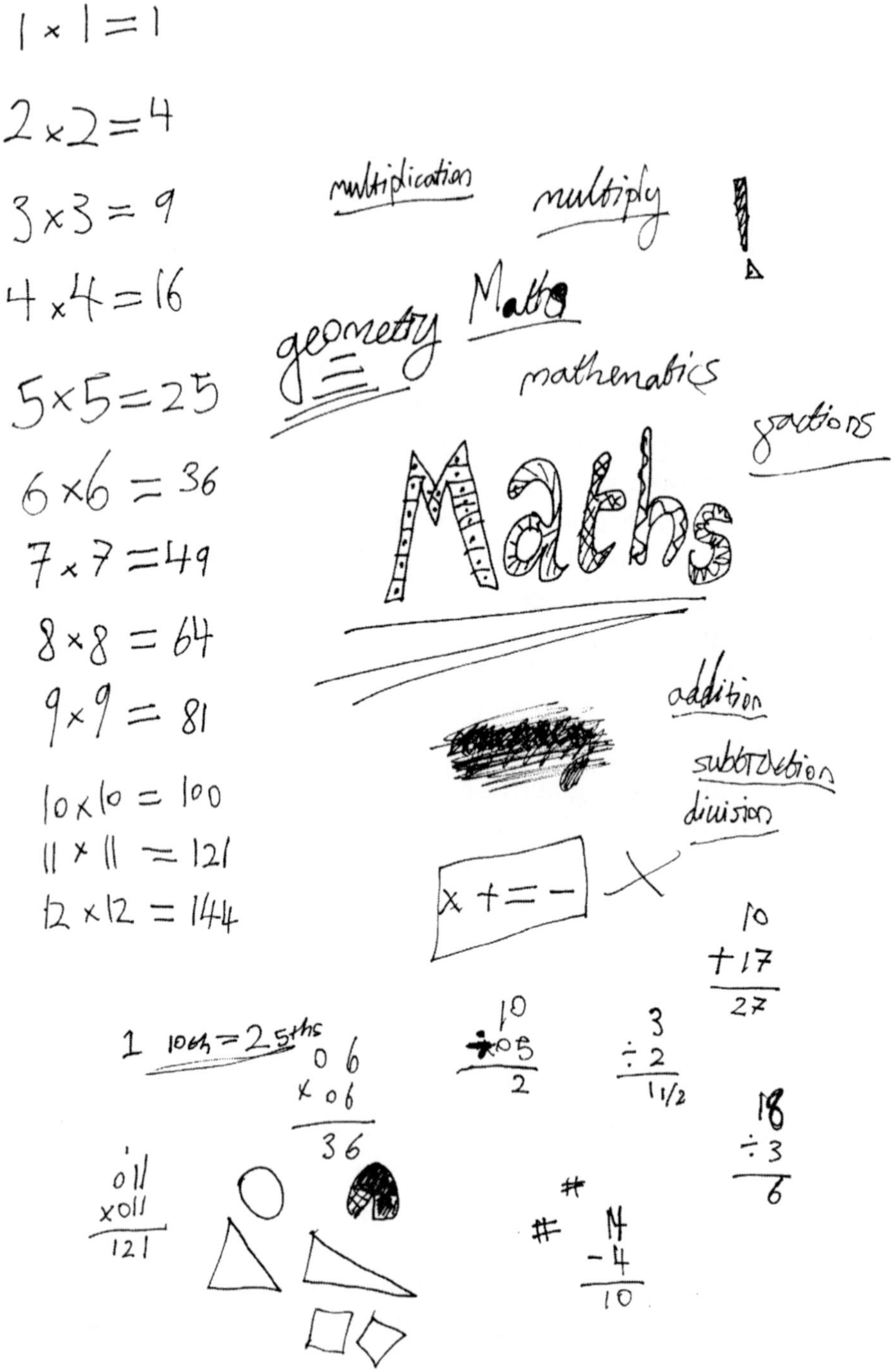

$1 \times 1 = 1$

$2 \times 2 = 4$

$3 \times 3 = 9$

$4 \times 4 = 16$

$5 \times 5 = 25$

$6 \times 6 = 36$

$7 \times 7 = 49$

$8 \times 8 = 64$

$9 \times 9 = 81$

$10 \times 10 = 100$

$11 \times 11 = 121$

$12 \times 12 = 144$

multiplication

multiply

geometry

Maths

mathematics

fractions

Maths

addition

subtraction

division

$x + = -$

$$10$$
$$+ 17$$
$$\overline{27}$$

$$1\ \tfrac{10th}{} = 2\ 5ths$$

$$06$$
$$\times 06$$
$$\overline{36}$$

$$10$$
$$\times 05$$
$$\overline{2}$$

$$3$$
$$\div 2$$
$$\overline{1\tfrac{1}{2}}$$

$$18$$
$$\div 3$$
$$\overline{6}$$

$$011$$
$$\times 011$$
$$\overline{121}$$

$$\#$$
$$\# \quad N$$
$$- 4$$
$$\overline{10}$$

Maths doodling by Bethany.

Maths

"Maths is beautiful."

~ Derek Robinson, brilliant baker of bread and raspberry muffins,
owner of Bluebell Bookshop, with a degree in Economics.

My friend Derek has a degree in Economics. He says maths is beautiful. I find it hard to believe, given my aversion to the subject, but I don't completely doubt that it truly is beautiful ~ if you can understand the song it sings. I also believe that the ancient art of sacred geometry has much to teach us.

Maths is the number one reason that parents baulk at home education. Because they aren't competent in maths, they fear their children won't be ~ which is an understandable concern.

I hate maths, and that's no understatement. Numbers make me nauseous. It's true! I feel a sense of vertigo at the thought of adding, or Pir^2, or fractions and roots. Numbers are of no interest to me, unless, of course, it's a cheque written favourably in my name; then, strangely, I can 'do the maths'.

In looking at maths books suitable for ten year olds, I realised that I clearly shut down to the subject well before that age. Yet here I am, navigating midlife both as a parent and as a woman with two publishing businesses, and what do you know? I'm still here! Even though I don't have high school level maths to my name, I don't feel remotely inadequate as a human being. Maths is simply unnecessary for my journey through life And many adults, if they're honest, will say that short of balancing their cheque book, the same applies to them. If maths is meant to be part of a person's life journey (and the same can be said of any subject), then the student will have a passion for it, and develop an understanding in a way that's not traumatic or reliant on a parent's skill in that area.

I've been publishing a magazine for eight years. A few years back, I was at the printing company, wanting to get some quotes. Pages are printed in lots of four, and I needed to get an idea. I can't remember what, exactly, but I asked the general manager what 7 x 8 was. He looked blank. Even though he's about five years older than me, and had a good British education, he didn't know 7 x 8, either! I felt rather smug for a good few seconds. You see, I could work out 7 x 8, and probably any other times table below 12, if I had about 20 – 30 seconds undisturbed time. He turned to his receptionist and asked her what 7 x 8 was. I couldn't believe it! Oops…another blank look! She got out her calculator! Honestly! Three intelligent, professional adults of a certain age, and none of us knew what we, as a culture, *expect* our kids to know! I learnt an awful lot that day, and certainly learnt to let go of expectations I may have had of my children doing maths.

My claim to shame in childhood was failing maths all the way through school. I came at the bottom of the class every time in exams. Completely predictable! I never expected a grade higher than an E (fail). And then, at age 15, I changed schools when I moved to South Australia, got a fabulous teacher, and then did maths based on real life situations. She liked me, used a different approach, and I, maths dunce of the century, got A ~ top of the class. I truly believe it was because it was taught in a way that I understood, rather than being all abstract and like an unknown language. When our learning style is catered for, I believe we're capable of learning anything. Sadly, a quarter of all children don't have their learning style catered for in mainstream education. My oldest daughter has one of those learning styles.

In my previous school, at age 14, I moved to year 11, where we had to choose between maths 1 and maths 2 (which was either very hard maths or pretty hard maths ~ it all seemed the same to me). You can imagine my horror, as I'd assumed by that age I'd not have to do maths at all. There was so much talk about senior school being to do with preparing for adulthood and choices, yet they weren't letting us choose whether to do maths or not! Well, forever the little rebel, I got myself a band of other students together, and we protested about having maths forced upon us when we were so 'old and apparently preparing for adulthood'! The school authorities buckled, and brought in another subject as an option. That subject was catering. I was thrilled, as I loved cooking. But you know, catering as a business isn't just about cooking. It's about maths! You've got to work out how much food to buy, and for how many people, and know how much to charge. You need to know percentages, fractions, ratios... Goodness! But you know what? It was real maths. I loved it, and got a distinction: top of the class. That subject was the joy of my whole high school education. And to this day, I love catering for large numbers of people.

Bethany has my physical reaction to maths. She says it gives her a headache even thinking about it. Bless her, I do understand. My own experience gives me the utmost empathy for her, and fortunately, it means that she's not ever going to have it forced down her throat. I'm conscious, though, of not ignoring it completely, and I'm able to ignite her interest in ways that don't make it feel like a subject. For example, when she was younger, I'd say to her, "Let's make a date and walnut loaf. Actually, let's make two. So, we'll need to double this recipe. Can you help me by writing up the shopping list with double the ingredients?" For some learning styles, like that of my daughter, imagining 150g of dates and multiplying it by two is a lot easier than 150 x 2. It's a very simple change to make in how information is both presented and interpreted.

A few years back, I needed to work out how much money to take to Ireland for a talk I was doing at the Home Educators' Network conference. The girls became part of the maths experience: we'll need x amount for petrol to the airport, y amount for the airport car park, z amount for food while we're there. Let's see, if I take £a from the bank, how much change will we have left? It just won't occur to Bethany that there's maths involved in the same way as if I wrote something like add up 45+ 35 + 70 and then subtract that from 200. This sort of maths is important for visual people. They can relate to it. Now, at almost 14, she teaches herself maths ~ when she feels like it.

Understanding your child's learning style ~ the way they process information ~ can make so much difference to your approach, and can take headaches out of any form of education. Watching Bethany learn over these past years has been an interesting experience. I can see how many elements of school would have been painfully difficult for her. This doesn't mean that she's not bright, or intelligent or capable of learning well: far from it. It's just that *how* she takes in information, processes it, and then communicates it, is vastly different from the majority of the population.

Bethany sees everything in colour, and when she's processing information it must correlate with that. So, if it's a sign, a letter, or word, it has a different colour. For example, the number one, is white, N is brown; E is lime green. Each word, name, month, season, day of the week has its own colour (or mixed colours ~ depending on which letters stand out). The first seven letters of the alphabet are shared with music, so they each have a colour when Bethany's playing her instruments.

Eliza and I share the same learning style. We both learn best by repetition ~ even though our personality type (which is also the same) abhors repetition. My husband's learning style is in a similar area to Eliza and I. When you have contrasts in a family, particularly between parents and children, it can make the challenges of formal education a nightmare, if they're not understood. I've been ever so thankful to have had a good understanding of these learning styles. (See *Learning Without Tears*, by Helyn Connerr.)

Understanding
your child's learning style
~ the way they process information ~
can make so much difference
to your approach,
and can take headaches
out of any form of education.

Competition

Just to return briefly to cooking as a school subject: I was always challenged by the competition element inherent in our Home Economics classes (as opposed to Catering classes). Who had the cleanest apron? Actually, who'd sewn the best apron for cooking class? Whose cake was the best? There really was very little joy in cooking. The pressure to perform had some of the more, let's just say, 'naughty' students secretly turning off the ovens of the more proficient bakers, so their cakes wouldn't cook in time before the end of the lesson. If your cake wasn't baked, you couldn't be marked. Knocking out some of the competition greatly increased the odds of 'success' for the rest of the class. Driven to crime and corruption because of a damn cake? It's ridiculous.

That bad girl who turned off the ovens? Yep, that was me. I'm hiding behind the keyboard in shame as I type! Michelle Verankamp, please forgive me!

One of my favourite places to be is in the kitchen, creating meals. My life's karma, though, is that although I love cooking and preparing meals, I'm an absolutely useless baker when it comes to making cakes. My Home Economics capers will haunt me forever. The Gods of Baking are determined to make me suffer. My family is used to my burnt cakes, my soggy cakes, my far from perfect cakes. They're very forgiving, and still, for reasons I'll never comprehend, would rather me bake a cake for their birthday than buy one. Many of my cakes have been turned into pudding ~ we just play make-believe!

It's a valuable lesson, though, in how to approach our own children's attempts at just about anything. Imagine, if you were in my shoes, and having cakes marked out of ten. They would probably always get between, ooooooooooooh, eight and nine out of ten for taste...but looks, texture, etc., would be oh, about two, every single time.

As adults, most people would simply rush to the supermarket, and avoid the torture. But this is what we do to children throughout their education! Call it cakes, call it maths, call it social studies. We mark everything. This is, then, how they measure themselves as a human being. What right have we to do this? Truly, what right? Do we ever look deep inside them to see what each grade has cost them in terms of self-esteem? Do we even think to look? I know of sisters who routinely got A in their report cards, but their mother's response was "Why didn't you get an A+?" Learning to cook, as an unschooler, doesn't carry the pressures of "who's made the best cake?" A cake is a cake for goodness sake! So why should any child be pressured into making something for the sake of a mark out ten? Surely the goal, if any, should be to enjoy the process of taking raw ingredients, and creating something you can enjoy with a cuppa tea?

Competition is rife in schools. Now personally, I don't have a problem with competition at any level if the people involved are there willingly and wholeheartedly, and having fun.

As a child, I always came last in my school running races. Well, a girl can only take so much humiliation before she becomes crafty! I soon learnt that I could avoid such trauma by skipping interschool sports days and heading down to the river with the schoolboys who were equally keen to avoid sporting events. I can tell you, swimming in the local river was way more fun!

I was a great swimmer, and often won school races. It felt wonderful. But can you see the difference? Competition is fine if we want to be part of it, and we don't mind winning or losing. How many people are happy if they come last? Our culture doesn't encourage 'losers', and nor do schools. My high school motto was: virtute et labore (only the best is good enough). Hmm, so what happens to those of us on the scrapheap of life who weren't 'the best'?

Learning to cook, as an unschooler, doesn't carry the pressures of "who's made the best cake?" A cake is a cake for goodness sake! So why should any child be pressured into making something for the sake of a mark out ten?

Literacy

I hear more and more people in broadcasting, with jobs as presenters, reporters and journalists, who don't have a grasp of grammar or diction.

Our local BBC Radio and ITV Border TV News, have reporters, journalists and presenters with a very poor grasp of the language, and extremely lazy diction. I often feel like I'm in a culture which is trying to dumb us all down. What example are these professionals giving to younger people? And I wonder what on Earth people are learning in schools, and at home, that this way of speaking is becoming normal.

Everywhere I go, I see the misuse of apostrophes ~ even in our library, of all places! Have they forgotten that they're educating all the children who walk through their doors?

I see the apostrophe catastrophe in supermarkets, big business, small shops and magazines. It's simply everywhere. People are putting apostrophes in plural words like 1920's or tea's, CD's, and, to my horror last week, there was a shop saying they are now open on Sunday's. Sundays with an apostrophe 's'? How can you go through ten or twelve years of *formal* education and not understand that an apostrophe doesn't occur in a plural, but is generally used to denote ownership (John's dog is big), or to show where a letter or letters have been omitted in a shortened word (I'm coming in when you're ready).

If school ~ as endorsed by the government ~ is so necessary to education and adult life, how is it that *so many people* seemed to have failed basic literacy?

This is the world our children are growing up in. My point is this: observe the world around you, and please stop fearing your child will end up in adulthood being a complete failure just because you didn't do lessons. If you're home educating, it won't happen!

If you take away anything from this book, let it be that the secret to good education is to let children follow their talents, and develop skills. It's such a gift to step back and stop controlling how and when they learn. We're ALWAYS learning: always learning. The key is for it to be fun; a game; a joy. It has to be child directed, not adult enforced. When we're travelling, my husband plays spelling. Eliza begs for hard words. I used to pick up any book of mine, fact or fiction, and just call out words, and the girls would spell them. I never stopped to think if it was suitable for their 'age'. I simply called out words. If they got it right, I told them. If they didn't, it was no big deal. I'd repeat the word, and spell it out. There was no shame involved. It's all about play. As soon as the person loses interest, we move on to something else. Hard as it might be to comprehend, this is a far more effective way of learning than to force a topic in the hope it will sink in through our determined efforts.

I was born with a need to absorb the written word. I read everywhere, to the point that if I don't have a book or magazine in the bathtub, I even read the labels on the shampoo bottles. Sad, but true. It's inevitable that my children have developed a love of reading. From their births, my head has been in one book or another. I usually have a few books on the go at once: a few by the bed, one or two near the bathtub, a couple by the laptop (waiting for dial-up to download pages), and the bookshelves are full.

As infants and young children, my girls' father read to them for hours every day. Professionally, he's made his income from his voice ~ as a broadcaster, singer, ventriloquist and voice-over for TV and radio. His voice has turned even the blandest children's stories ~ and I can tell you there are a lot of them ~ into something interesting and fun for the whole family. My fondest Winter memory is him reading to us as a family, every night by the fire, from The Secret Garden, using a Yorkshire accent.

Not once have my husband and I ever sat down and attempted to teach our children to read. We never had to. Somewhere around the age of seven, when they were losing their milk teeth, they started to pick up very simple books, and would ask what certain words were. And in a matter of weeks, both of them, in their own time, went from simple Ladybird books, to reading novels. Out of everything that has happened in unschooling, this has, for me, been the most amazing. Out of seemingly nowhere, my two children, who were never taught to read, suddenly read books! I'm still in awe of this, really. I'd never have believed it was possible, had I not witnessed it myself. And it's a perfect example of the key to unschooling. It's about trusting the evolution and growth of our children. I can, however, see *how* they learnt to read. They watched, they absorbed, they participated by listening. They spent a lot of time immersed in books (still do) ~ both fiction and non-fiction, each interested in their chosen topics: for example, romance, vampires, animals, history, the Solar System.

I'm always struck, when they read something out loud to me, how fluent their reading is; how sound their comprehension is; and just as interesting, to me, how expressively they read.

I've heard many people, young and old, read in a monotone, with no light or shade; yet from the earliest stage of their reading, my daughters seemed to grasp how to express words. And this is because they felt the words; breathed words; heard words which were expressed in that way; and saw how words were lifted off the page, and life breathed into them. Words were living entities.

Watching the evolution of them being read to, to becoming readers, has taught me more about unschooling than anything else has. Children will learn if the fire is there, and if we trust them to do so.

Eliza's early spelling.

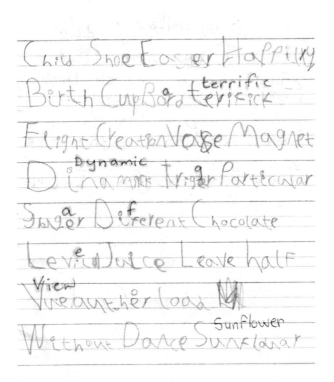

Watching the evolution of them being read to, to becoming readers, has taught me more about unschooling than anything else has.

*You might well wonder what use I am to a child
who wants to learn about history.*

*Again, this is a perfect example of
stepping out of the way
when it comes to 'how children learn'.*

Eliza on the beach, Rimini, Italy. Aged six.

Once Upon A Time

Even the word, 'history', has an effect on me not dissimilar to maths. Don't get me wrong, I don't have a complete aversion to things of the past. I enjoy watching the TV series *Who Do You Think You Are?*, which traces the genealogy of celebrities, and I'm fascinated with anything about the lost lands of Atlantis and Lemuria. I don't even mind reading the occasional historical novel, but that's probably where history starts and ends for me. You might well wonder what use I am to a child who wants to learn about history. Again, this is a perfect example of stepping out of the way when it comes to 'how children learn'.

Through my study of psychological astrology, I've learnt that Eliza has Venus in Capricorn in the 5th house. What this means is that Venus, the planet of love (what we love, who we love and what we attract and value) is, for her, in the sign of Capricorn, which is ruled by Saturn. Saturn is all about the old and traditional. It's very much about history! The fifth house of astrology is about our creativity (also children, love affairs, entertainment and gambling). So, for this daughter of mine, it's only natural that she'd love exploring history. It's something that genuinely brings her pleasure. She's expressed a strong interest in acting in historical dramas, too.

I failed history throughout school, until the last year. It's interesting to me that I always succeeded in subjects where I had a wonderful emotional rapport with the teacher, regardless of the subject. It just so happened that the teachers I gelled with the most were in the humanities.

In hindsight, I see that these teachers created a safe space for me to learn. I received an A, top mark, for Asian history in my last year of school. I remember not a fact or story about any of it. I'd failed, or just scraped a pass, for all my other years of history, covering different cultures and countries throughout time. As someone with a distaste for such things, what positive influence could I possibly be for my daughters? As Laura Ingalls, who shares my dislike, remarked in Little House on the Prairie: "History's all about dead people."

Eliza's depth and knowledge of history astounds me. I often look at her father with eyes which ask 'Where did she learn that?' Her memory of dates and events seems photographic. She learnt about planets in the same way. She could tell you far more about the weight, measurements and other facts of planetary life than I ever could. Equally, when I introduced her to astrology, she picked it up instantly. She did this not only with facts, but also intuitively.

Eliza's translating her love of history into her love for creative, fiction writing, and I'd be very surprised if at some point in her life she wasn't working professionally as a historical novelist, or at least enjoying it as a dedicated hobby. She's started a few novels in this genre, and is currently working on one about someone called Missouri Riddle.

All humans who are not under inordinate hardship have topics they're passionate about, and ones that mean nothing to them. Our role as parents is to find ways for our children to discover what they love and don't love, and then to get right out of their way. *That's the greatest educational gift we can present.* If we can support their journey, such as buying or borrowing books on history, or visiting museums, then that's icing on the cake. We certainly don't need to sit down with text books, and teach them. If they want to learn it, they will.

For Eliza, a visit to the village of Sedbergh in the Yorkshire Dales (about an hour from here), is heaven. This village is made up of lots of second hand bookshops. She adores searching through the old books, and has bought herself a fairy tale book that's 118 years old.

As a saxophonist, she can learn about the lives of famous saxophone players of the past. As an unschooler, she has oodles of free time to study this, for as long as she likes. Her learning isn't curtailed because of a class bell. She can do it in her own time, when she feels like it. She's not dependent on 30 other children having to study this topic, nor will she miss out on it if it's not on the National Curriculum.

Her learning isn't curtailed
because of a class bell.
She can do it in her own time,
when she feels like it.
She's not dependent on 30 other children
having to study this topic,
nor will she miss out on it
if it's not on the National Curriculum.

Philosophy

Unschooling is a philosophy, and certainly a philosophical approach to life. It teaches us to ask questions: not just the children, but the parents, too. For this reason, it can be very hard to actually write or talk about what it means, because it's so personal. Some of the philosophical questions which unschooling throws up include:

Who are the real experts in a child's learning experience?

Why do we believe that children must be with other people's children every day in order to learn to be their innately social selves?

If we didn't have any books, computers or other technology, would our children be deprived?

Do I expect my child to know what they'll do with the 'rest of their life' by the time she or he is a teenager, and why?

If I take away all the traditional measuring sticks of education, what am I left with?

What is it that terrifies me so much about being with my children 24/7?

If we're teaching our children about responsibility, then why do we abdicate most of that responsibility by sending our children to school?

What do I want most for my children? Can that only be found in school?

Why do I want/expect my children to be academically successful? Who is that desire for: them or me? Why?

Regardless of the weather or the season,
we do well to employ Nature
on a daily basis.
It's in the depths of Mother Nature,
that we tap into our creative, genius self.

Veronika and Bethany, Spring 2002, Addingham churchyard cemetery, Glassonby

The One Income Family

Many home educators are on a low budget or single income. It's almost inevitable, because, by its nature, you need a stay-at-home parent, and someone else to earn the income. Strangely enough, this is actually, more often than not, to our children's advantage, because the income is likely to be treated as a precious resource. When we have slim resources, our ability to develop imagination and creativity seems to increase enormously.

Many, many years ago, I worked as a nanny for a rather rich family. The ironic thing was they never had food in the house! Somehow I was expected to create a meal for a family of four on little more than potatoes and tinned tuna. I have to say, as a young woman of about 19, this really bugged me. I liked to be able to pick and choose ingredients, to have variety: essentially, to be able to play in the kitchen.

I grew up in a house of eight children. Our cupboards and fridge were always full to overflowing. Each week, my mum travelled to a town called Stanthorpe, famous for an annual apple and grape festival. Mother would stock up on all our fruit and vegetables from there. We had boxes of grapes, apples, potatoes, carrots and so on, not to mention the foods growing in the garden.

In many ways, the whole Mother Hubbard's bare cupboard scenario of the family I'd worked for actually helped me to become a more imaginative cook. I didn't know that was happening until much later in my life. And it's the same with our children. Although it's great to have all sorts of resources at our disposal, they're not actually that necessary. Because of my experience nannying for that family, I'm now able to rustle up meals from next to nothing…the same sparse ingredients would have most people racing to their nearest shop.

If you could only have one resource to use as an unschooling family, then I'd suggest using Nature. Forget books, videos, the Internet or museums, and go for a walk in the woods, beach, marshland, rainforest. Even if you live in the world's largest city, there are still parklands to explore. Nature is always changing. She always has new gifts to show us, if only we take the time to look, smell, hear and feel. Every day of the year her face is different. Regardless of the weather or the season, we do well to employ Nature on a daily basis. It's in the depths of Mother Nature, that we tap into our creative, genius self. I also believe that it's healthy for all humans to develop skills and a sense of inner discipline in practising to become proficient in a particular interest, whether it's learning a musical instrument, a language, yoga, dancing, tending plants, writing poetry, life drawing, sacred geometry…

My girls are now teaching themselves to play guitar and ukulele. They saved up for these instruments, and the desire to learn is strong. I can't afford any more music lessons on top of the saxophone, piano and violin, so they have to be disciplined and use the musical skills they have to develop their playing ability on these new instruments.

It's about learning to live simply,
and feeling abundant regardless of our income level.
It's about feeling wealth in the joy of life,
not in the material trappings that humans
surround themselves with.
A healthy and wholesome life develops
from within ourselves,
not from a shopping catalogue or excessive expense.

Home Educating On A Low Income

Spring, 2005 ~ The Mother magazine, Issue 5

I'm often asked how we manage to home educate on a low family income, with just one parent working. We made a choice to have one parent stay at home from birth anyway, so adapting to one income isn't a new thing. From my experience, I don't think the question is so much about 'how do you live on one income and home educate?' but 'how do you live on one income and raise kids?' For our family, it's about learning to live simply, and feeling abundant regardless of our income level. It's about feeling wealth in the joy of life, not in the material trappings that humans surround themselves with. A healthy and wholesome life develops from within ourselves, not from a shopping catalogue or excessive expense.

Here are some ideas that might prove helpful, regardless of your current income level. Remember, home education is a lifestyle choice, and shouldn't be separated from the rest of your life.

[] Buy wholefoods in bulk through a Workers' Cooperative, such as Suma Wholefoods. Learn to eat simply. Avoid ready-made meals. They not only cost you a small fortune, but they cost the environment in many unseen ways. Teaching your children how to prepare food is a valuable skill, as well as an art. Enjoy eating together (without the TV on), and precede your meal with a blessing of gratitude. Bring mindfulness to your mealtimes. You'll eat slowly, and not as much, because your brain will have had time to register that your stomach is full.

[] Reduce, reuse, recycle ~ and I'll add another one: refuse. Think about what that really means. Be honest with your children about the part that each of us plays in the destruction and/or healing of this Earth. You don't always have to buy new things. Learn to say 'no'.

[] Have one family car, or use public transport/walk/car share.

[] Get rid of the TV. This has many bonuses. It'll save you the cost of the TV licence. The children won't be sucked into brainwashing schemes. Children will be creative, and need less in their life, not more.

[] Turn off the lights when you're not in the room.

[] Grow soft fruits, and vegetables, in your garden. Permaculture allows you to get an amazing yield per square foot. Try it and see!

Save your seeds from last year's harvest, and watch your children embrace the pleasures of creating a family food supply. You can really reduce your food bill by multi-cropping, and eating botanically (low on the food chain). No garden? Grow a variety of sprouts on your windowsill.

[] Do you really need such a big house? And do the children really need a bedroom each?

[] Put a small amount of money away each week for using towards resources, birthdays and other celebrations. Just £10 a week adds up to £520 a year. That buys a lot of books, gifts, wooden toys, excursions, even a family camping holiday to explore a new area.

[] Consider learning skills for yourself so you can share them with the children, rather than paying professional tuition fees. For example, you could learn a new language. Libraries stock language books and CDs.

[] Most people can teach themselves the basics of music. We were fortunate enough to buy an old piano for £30. These days, they're often given away on Freecycle or Freegle. Our piano needed a tune up, but it's got a lovely tone.

[] Libraries often have free access to the Internet for school-age children. You don't need to have it at home.

[] Encourage your children to have pen pals. This opens up an amazingly huge world for them, and develops their writing and communication skills in other areas, such as geography, history and culture.

[] Register with Museums and National Parks, for student discounts.

[] Order stationery, and craft/music supplies through discount suppliers, at wholesale prices. You might like to team up with a friend to order.

[] Buy second hand books. Borrow books.

[] All of life is an education. Turn every excursion, no matter how short or simple, into a learning experience incorporating multiple senses. A walk to the woods or along the seashore can be a rich learning experience that needn't cost a bean.

[] There are bound to be people you know, maybe an elderly person, who'd delight in sharing a skill or talent, such as knitting, cabinet making or dancing. We had a friend show us how to make our own charcoal pencils for artwork. He collected elderflower twigs from our garden, trimmed them, and cooked them in an old children's paint tin, in our fireplace. Half an hour later, voila! Our own charcoal sticks. It saved a trip to town, the girls found it interesting, and now they know how to make their own.

Bethany and Eliza are delighted to have their grandmother Angelikah living with them again. She's teaching the girls German.

[] Write a resource list of what you'd like for home education. Pin it up for all to see. Watch in wonder as these things manifest into your life. My guess is that very little of it will need to be purchased. Got a commercial printer in town, or some friendly business people who'll pass on leftover paper? It doesn't take long to change the habit of always needing an unused bit of paper. Envelopes and scraps of paper can be used over and over again. I do spend a bit more on some products, like Ferby pencils. They're good quality, eco-friendly pencils that not only feel nice for the child to hold, but also produce beautiful colour on the page. They don't break easily, and are worth every penny. They're long lasting. Once you've tried these, you won't go back to cheap pencil offers of 50 for £1.

Your day-to-day life provides rich learning. Enjoy it, and let go of the feeling that you need a virtual university in your home. You don't. It's up to each of us, as holistic parents, to break away from this society obsessed with instant gratification. If it takes a day or two for your child to find the answer to a question about why certain animals have spots, or the impact of melting ice caps, that's ok. Let it be ok. They'll become more balanced people as a result. And finally, remember, there's no price on laughter.

Bethany at Lacey's Caves, Little Salkeld.

When we hear a story,
the majority of neural fields in the brain
are activated.
When a child watches television,
only one field is in use.

Maraetai Beach, Auckland, New Zealand:
Paul and Bethany learning about the water.

TV or Not TV?

"Ralph Waldo Emerson once asked what we would do if the stars only came out once every thousand years. No one would sleep that night, of course. The world would create new religions overnight. We would be ecstatic, delirious, made rapturous by the glory of God. Instead, the stars come out every night and we watch television."
~ Paul Hawkon.

Amongst unschoolers, there seem to be two quite different approaches to the subject of television. Some families allow their kids unlimited access to TV, taking a libertarian approach to all aspects of life, including unlimited access to sugar and junk food. I don't believe this is healthy, because *all* children need to understand that this Earthly life does contain limitations, and every action has a consequence.

In our home, the girls were raised without TV. They saw the odd bit when away at their Nana's house, or on holiday. Why did we take this approach? It actually began about the time I was getting ready to birth my second child, Eliza. We'd been letting Bethany watch 'Barney' (you know, the hideous purple dinosaur!) and she was glued to the TV. This gave me a chance to have a lie-in in the mornings with my new baby. My husband then had the idea of recording it, so Bethany could watch it again later. Children learn very quickly, and soon she was demanding Barney over and over again. It became an obsession. I'm very thankful I had the foresight to see what was happening, rather than continuing its use as a babysitter, which would have been far easier to do. At the time, I had *no* idea of the deleterious effects of TV. I was just a young mum who observed something rather unhealthy developing, and trusted my intuition.

One day, I said that the TV had to go. So we hid it in the cupboard, and a week later finally got rid of it. It's one of the best parenting decisions we've ever made. I'm not going to deny that television is an important source of information. But it's also a distraction from living, and it's the latter that we've guarded against as parents.

There are some fundamental differences between children and adults, and one of them is that children are still developing. And this difference applies to how we view a television. All children suffer from watching television, because it stops movement, and poorly stimulates the senses. When I described Bethany earlier as a toddler being glued to the television, that pretty well sums up what happens when any child watches the screen. They don't get to scan the picture or practise eye/hand co-ordination, tend not to ask questions, or explore topics. They don't practise gross or fine motor skills. Initiation and motivation aren't needed. Creativity and analytical thinking are suppressed. TV doesn't promote logical thinking, because of the manner in which TV programmes are made.

Before televisions, parents were more likely to occupy their children by storytelling. When we hear a story, the majority of neural fields in the brain are activated. When a child watches television, only one field is in use. Without going into scientific jargon, what essentially happens is that the brain is *anaesthetised* when we watch television.

When our girls were 11 and 9, we introduced a TV into our home so they could watch a programme on volcanoes, and another on weather patterns. What struck me was that, very much like taking them to the movies, they talked non-stop, asking all sorts of questions! This is not common amongst school children and children raised on a daily diet of television. We've set firm boundaries around TV use, both in terms of content, and the number of hours watched per week.

All children **suffer** *from watching television because it stops movement, and poorly stimulates the senses.*

Rugged up for a Wintry walk.

Creatures of Habit

The habits we have as adults are witnessed by our children. This first came home to me long before I became a *biological* parent. I worked in a Steiner Boarding School for intellectually disabled teenagers, in New Zealand, as a dormitory parent. My job included making meals, looking after the teenagers outside of school time, and tending to the house we lived in. There were a few dormitory parents for each house.

Now, for most of my life, I've tended to eat my meals just using my fork. I don't know why, perhaps it's just laziness. My parents certainly don't eat like this, but I've noticed my older sister does, so maybe I picked it up from her when I was a child. I use a knife in restaurants or at other people's houses, but not in my own home. About a week after I started at the boarding school, one of the dormitory parents asked me to use my knife. I was a little put out, until he pointed to EVERY teenager around the table. They were all eating their meals in the same way as me! (Whether humans should be taught to use cutlery is another matter altogether). It won't surprise you to know that my own children have picked up this habit.

Habits, of course, aren't just 'bad' things. They're anything we tend to do without thinking or which becomes automatic. Our job as parents is to foster good and healthy, life-enriching and nurturing habits for our children to emulate, and one of the most significant acts that we demonstrate is the way we relate to the child's other parent.

There are the obvious habits, like brushing teeth; but what about the not so obvious ones, like taking adequate daily exercise, fresh air, and drinking plenty of water? And living with a sense of orderliness or gratitude? These, to me, are as vital to education and learning as knowing the core subjects as ordained by the government.

Our learning journey, at some level, involves other people. I remember as a child in school, at one point being a teacher's pet ~ adored for being full of life, vitality, and thinking outside the box. And yet, other teachers simply thought I was a little trouble maker, hell on legs, and they truly 'hated' me. I could feel it. Imagine being in that energy field all day long? I'm not surprised that 25 years later I'm writing about the value of not sending your children to school. The prophecies we inflict on our children are based on their grades.

Every time they're sent home with a report card, these measurements paint a picture to the child, and to the world, of their value as a human being. When I became an adult, and worked in classroom settings at a Montessori school, I knew the pleasure and prejudice of having a teacher's pet. First, there's that adorable, cherubic creature that you secretly hope will be cloned when you have your own children. And then there are the other little humans: such as the child you find it hard to imagine any parent loving ~ a sour, squinty-eyed and vicious terror. She's the one who needs even more love.

In school, we have no say in how teachers perceive our children. What we might think of as cute or endearing in our child, could well be the thing that drives a teacher to a new career! Likewise, the aspects about our children which most challenge us, could well be admired by a long-suffering teacher who can see clearly into the future.

Even though our children can range between both extremes, the difference between them and school children is that when they're with us, we love them no matter how sour, nasty or horrid their *behaviour* might be on a given day. We love them whether or not they're having a bad day. And that's the secret of the unschooling family. No matter how difficult any day is, we have glue that binds us together, which a school teacher doesn't have with his/her pupils, no matter how kind and well intentioned s/he is.

Love is the basis of the unschooling lifestyle, and is without doubt the motivating factor for choosing unschooling in the first place. Something that's often overlooked in education is the relationship between children and adults, and the authoritarian attitude most teachers take. In our experience, because our girls' opinions are valued and respected, they're often taken aback by adults outside the home who treat them with disrespect or as if their opinions aren't valid. If this is the norm in schools, then neither child nor adult will tend to question such injustices.

Intimacy

I don't think I ever truly appreciated the intimacy of our family life until my daughters chose to 'try out' school, when Bethany was 11 and Eliza, nine.

It didn't take long for them to start coming home as strangers. Who were these people getting off the school bus with their bad attitudes, rude tone, and lack of affection? They weren't the daughters I'd spent the last decade with.

Each day that they were immersed in school, they lost a piece of their essential selves. Each day that they sat in an environment which didn't honour their true potential, and each day they existed in a place where they couldn't be their *true* selves, they became less of the people I'd grown to know and love over the years. As a parent, I felt powerless to change this, and to *support* them. My influence was now very small. After all, they were away from home 8am – 4pm, and their home time was spent doing homework, eating and sleeping.

Family life was eroding. Is this how other families live *all the time*? Does the government want schooling to begin so early in a child's life that parents have no idea what's happening, and how much they're missing out on; so early, that they see their child's 'schooled' behaviour as normal?

There's a natural intimacy that lives within the heart of an unschooling family, and it exists because of the close physical proximity to each family member on a daily basis.

The human aura spreads out several feet, and 'bumps' into other auras nearby. This is the reason we can suddenly become tired, sad or rejuvenated when around others. Imagine your child in school all day, mingling with the auras of 30 to 300 (or even more) other children, and teachers ~ each one bringing their own energy, agendas, pain or health issues to the cultural soup of school. Imagine that each day your child is immersed in this, and each day your child brings a bit of this back into your home.

Many families resonate with the idea of school because it creates an instant pseudo-community ~ and community is something sadly lacking in our culture. Community, however, comes with its own set of rules, guidelines and belief systems. When your child is in school, they come away with an investment in those belief systems, because,

Eliza and Bethany, out in the village. Below: Bethany and Veronika

without them, they'll not survive in the pseudo-community. No-one enjoys feeling like an outcast, so we either learn to shut up and hide our true feelings and beliefs, or disappear into the sunset. It's not easy for children to do that when they're in the school 'soup' day in and day out.

When my children decided to come out of school (they began in March, and were out by that October), it took several months to see their 'old selves' returning. Their innocence had been lost, and they've never fully returned to the children I knew. I'm reconciled to this, as it was also an important part of their lives to follow the desire to try out school, and for me to trust their choice. They've discovered it isn't remotely as interesting or as fun as they imagined it might be ~ we'll blame Harry Potter for giving them the idea of it being the best place on Earth.

The girls also learnt that sometimes information taught in schools isn't accurate or correct. They've had to balance this with somehow respecting the voice of authority, and knowing their place in the pecking order! Even if a teacher is wrong, there's no room to disagree without being labelled as rude, a trouble maker or other derogatory title.

For a long time, Eliza's had a great interest in food ~ not only eating it, but making meals, and learning about the origins of recipes and cultural dishes, as well as nutritional content. She'd come home amazed at the nutrition taught in school, and how outdated the information was. My eyes would nearly pop out when reading what was being served in the school canteen on 'healthy eating' days. What were they eating on other days?

Needless to say, my children always took lunch from home. Near the end of their school days, when it was obvious neither of them was happy, I asked them what they loved about school so much that was keeping them there. When they replied: "The lunches you give us", I nearly fell over laughing. "But you can eat those at home every single day!"

The lunch hall was an interesting learning environment. First, those who had school lunches weren't allowed to sit with children who brought packed ones. School lunches were served on plastic trays with built-in dish, plate and cutlery compartments. There's nothing beautiful or inviting about this, nor the environment they're forced to sit in. The children didn't have the freedom to sit outside under a tree or on the grass to eat their food, but instead, had to listen to the noise of dozens of others while they ate. Compare this to lunch at home: we begin with grace, to give thanks for the food which has grown; our meals are eaten from pottery or wooden plates or bowls; a candle is lit; there are flowers on the table; and conversations with those we love.

Eliza came home off the school bus every day with a rotten headache. I'm not surprised. At morning and afternoon tea, they weren't even allowed to sit down, but had to stand with all the other children in the hallway, where the bags and coats were. I'll bet the teachers didn't eat their snacks in that sort of environment.

Even if a teacher is wrong,
there's no room to disagree
without being labelled as rude,
a trouble maker or other derogatory title.

School bus, drawn by Bethany.

The Artisan Bakery

On the cooling rack in our tiny, cerise pink kitchen, sits a loaf of freshly baked sourdough rye bread with caraway seeds sprinkled on top. This is a favourite in our home. I've modelled it on the rye bread of my childhood with German parents. The memories are warm, safe and loving. They remind me of early mornings, when my dad and I would leave our suburban home in Brisbane, and drive the two hours into the country, where we'd bought a farm at Freestone, on the Darling Downs: and where we'd soon live for many years. They're definitely 'feel-good' memories.

The sourdough starter was given to me by a friend from Ireland. Sourdough works by using a 'starter' of fermented dough as a leaven, rather than yeast, to raise the bread. Whenever the dough is made and kneaded, a handful is taken out and put into the fridge to be used for the next loaf.

Sourdough bread making is a mindful practice and art. It can't be rushed. It epitomises the slow life. The evening before baking the bread, the starter is taken from the fridge, and mixed with a little flour and warm water: and then left covered overnight to start fermenting some more. In the morning, more flour and warm water are added, and the dough kneaded. The mixture's left for a few hours to rise, somewhere warm, before being baked.

Commercially-made bread (and most home-baked breads) use quick acting yeast to produce bread in a hurry. The bread is then packaged in plastic, to be sold to the hungry public. If 'plastic' sliced bread is all you've ever known, you could find the taste of a good old fashioned loaf of home-baked bread ~ especially our delicious sourdough rye bread ~ not to be to your taste at all. Likewise, if you've grown up with top quality bread ~ a bread made with the hands of love ~ you'll be unmoved, if not repulsed, by what the masses consume on a daily basis: what, for some, is a staple food.

I can't help but contrast the unschooled life with our home-baked bread. The pace of our days is slow. The style of our education is not 'quick acting yeast' used with the purpose of a 'one size fits all' learning agenda. There are no 'uniform' loaves.

Just as each loaf of bread that we make is different from the last, so too is our learning, and our learning styles. Our life as a bakery is warm, productive, but oh so very artisan! Just as the steam from the oven warms our home, so too, does the intimacy and interaction of our family community. By baking our sourdough, we're connected to what we're putting inside ourselves. And the same is to be said of our unschooling. We feel the raw ingredients in our hands, the warmth of the water as we're kneading. Time is taken to let the mixture do what it needs to do, namely, grow. The steam from the oven is all around our faces. We're part of the life of the bread.

When we consume commercial bread, we're not connected. We haven't picked up the flour from the local watermill where it's been freshly stone-ground, or felt the dough in our hands. We've not bided our time, patiently doing other things, while allowing the process of rising to occur. We've not enjoyed the smell that comes from freshly baked bread on the work top. The bread we bake ourselves not only tastes different, it is different. We've even eaten it with mindfulness. How many people who eat sliced, 'plastic' bread, stop and say "I can really feel the heart and soul of the baker"?

Mainstream education can be likened to sliced, 'plastic' bread. It's the same recipe, every time, regardless of who it's for. In general, there's no mindfulness for the individual child, and their soul needs. It uses quick acting yeast and works to a static formula regardless of the 'feel of the day'. As a home-baker, it's important to be in the right mood to bake. I learnt this many years ago, when working in a Steiner Boarding school. We all took turns to bake bread. Mine was always different to everyone else's! Not bad, or better, just different. It had real life to it, but it also changed depending on the day of the week, the phases of the Moon, and how I was feeling within myself.

Mainstream education is formulaic, not artisan like the bread baked with our own hands.

I can't help but contrast the unschooled life
with our home-baked bread.
The pace of our days is slow.
The style of our education is not
'quick acting yeast'
used with the purpose of a
'one size fits all' learning agenda.
There are no 'uniform' loaves.

Paul bringing in the firewood on a snowy Winter's day.

Feeding the Fire

Our old sandstone cottage was built in 1678, and apparently was originally a stable. The terraced cottage on one side of us was once the village post office.

To heat our home in Winter relies on some rather manual labour. There's no switching on the central heating when it gets cold. There is no central heating! We have two open fireplaces, one of which is useless and not worth lighting.

The wood which crackles in the hearth of our home all Autumn and Winter is grown in the village. The local forester sells us what's known as slab wood. This is the so-called waste wood that's not used for building. He delivers it on a trailer, and then Paul saws and chops it up to make it the right size for our fireplace. It's the girls' task to bring in baskets of wood, regardless of whether it's snowing or blowing a gale. There's mindfulness about being connected to the trees which have grown on the hills around us, and now warm our bodies.

The consciousness of using a renewable resource, like wood, and chopping our own kindling, rather than buying it from a shop, is akin to the unschooling life. It would be easy to use the kerosene-based firelighters (National Curriculum) to ignite our fire, but we choose wax and wood-based lighters, or dried pine cones (Natural Curriculum). It's a simple change, but it makes all the difference when you don't have to breathe in toxic fumes, pollute the environment (the one 'out there', or the internal one), but can live freely.

Unlike coal or wood stoves, open fires need constant feeding. They must be tended, and with care. So too, does the human imagination. Our curiosity must be fed, tended and nurtured. There's a complete cycle to burning wood: the trees must grow, be felled, chopped, carried into the home, and burnt. The ashes go onto the garden, and nourish more life. The cycle continues. This connection to the world around us is at the heart of the unschooling life.

Unlike coal or wood stoves,
open fires need constant feeding.
They must be tended, and with care.
So too, does the human imagination.
Our curiosity must be fed,
tended and nurtured.

Grenzy and the Mona Lisa (aka Eliza) enjoy each other's company by the fireside.

Paul likes to remind us of the great Zen saying:
"Before enlightenment,
chop wood, carry water.
After enlightenment,
chop wood, carry water."

I wonder if Zen masters had chainsaws...

Our girls have grown up with stories.
Even before they could speak,
we told them stories.
Even after they could read fluently,
themselves, we told them stories.
We still do.

*Dad reading us stories, illustrated by
Bethany.*

The Cantadora

Storytelling and stories are important forms of medicine, as well as entertainment, and an ancestral passing of knowledge. When author and cantadora, Clarissa Pinkola Estes, went to work at Columbine High School the day after the massacre, and for the next three years, she discovered that most of the teenagers there not only didn't know how to pray (they'd never been shown), they hadn't been told stories as children. Is this the price this generation has paid for the benefit of the 'working mom' and cable television?

Storytelling is as old as humanity. Even before we had words to speak, we used pictures and music to tell stories. Medicine, music, history, magic, meaning ~ all these have been passed down, generation by generation, by storytelling elders. And now they're becoming extinct?

Our girls have grown up with stories. Even before they could speak, we told them stories. Even after they could read fluently, themselves, we told them stories. We still do.

In our valley, there's a group of storytellers which meets in the local independent bookshop. This is a safe space where people can come to listen to stories; they don't have to tell any, unless they want to. Occasionally, a guest storyteller comes along. One of our favourites was a Navajo Indian with all sorts of amazing stories and music.

We each have stories within, waiting to be told, waiting for ears to hear. There's a skill, as well as an art, to listening to stories, as well as being able to recount them with our own character etched into the words.

We're blessed, here in the Eden Valley, to be connected to the visiting rural scheme which brings storytellers and musicians to the village halls in the area.

The Soup Kitchen

Recently, I attended two group events where I brought soup to share. The first was Moroccan chickpea soup: chickpeas and vegetables in a rich, tomatoey sauce, with cinnamon and apricots. The other soup was pumpkin, also with cinnamon. On both occasions, people were asking me what the spice was. They knew it was something familiar, but they couldn't place it because it was out of context, not where they expected it to be.

The reaction was always the same: "I would *never* think to put cinnamon into a savoury dish." The soups were enjoyed, despite (or because of) this unexpected ingredient. It's a fine lesson, though, in thinking outside the box, and in using resources to create things with a twist.

Soup is, essentially, vegetables and/or grains, and water, with some herbs, spices or other seasoning. My family will tell you that I never make the same soup twice. The reason for this is that I don't measure ingredients, and rarely follow recipes. When I make soup, I make soup for the soul, and from the soul, whether it's creamy onion and potato; thick and rich minestrone; creamy cauliflower; pumpkin and cinnamon with toasted sage and rye bread croutons on top; parsnip, nutmeg and apple; roast red pepper and garlic; or good ol' lentil and smoked tofu hotpot!

A friend recently said that if she served her husband soup for dinner, he'd make a fuss: he'd not been at work all day to come home to 'soup'. I dropped a pot of soup off for their dinner one night; he was most delighted at the meal which awaited him. Cheeky thing! I don't see soup as a poor man's meal, but a delicious delight for the senses.

Unschooling days are like my home-made vegetable soups. There's no recipe to follow. The ingredients are always different. Some days the Sun is shining, and everyone is keen to get out of bed and have some fun, to go on an adventure. Other times, there's a gale force wind threatening at the window pane. The thick, pewter clouds menace their way into the middle of the village. This is a duvet and hot chocolate sort of day, and no one is going to get in the way of that! It's no less of a day than a bright, sunny, race outside sort of morning after drinking freshly made vegetable juice; but it has a different energy, and that's what we respond to. Sometimes, especially when the weather persists in being dreary, there's nothing for it but to escape our cabin fever, and to don our brightest clothes, and seek an adventure outside the home. Maybe it's a trip to the beautiful Yorkshire dales to browse in one of the many second-hand book shops in the village of Sedbergh. Or perhaps we'll go to an animal rescue centre, and say 'hi' to the unloved creatures. Will we adopt one? Maybe we'll go to the movies, or a café.

I adore soup, and never tire of it. And the reason is because, unlike soup from a tin or packet, my soups are always different, and made with love and joy. I adore unschooling for this reason, too. Every day is unique. Some are quiet; some active and a little frantic and unpredictable.

The thick, pewter clouds
menace their way
into the middle of the village.
This is a duvet and hot chocolate sort of day,
and no one is going to get in the way of that!

*Our family
planted hundreds of fruit trees.
It was a snowy,
achingly bitter Winter's day...*

Fruit Forest

Human beings are designed to live between the tropics of Capricorn and Cancer: a lovely warm, tropical niche. Within this environment we once lived in fruit forests, satiating the hormonal needs of our large brain by daily consumption of perfectly ripe fruit. No such joy in temperate England! I grew up in sub-tropical Queensland, with the exquisite flavour and nectar of mango etched into my soul forever. Fruit is such a gift from this Earth. In England, the vast majority of commercial orchards have been grubbed out to make way for raising cattle and growing wheat.

In February 2004, our family planted hundreds of fruit trees. It was a snowy, achingly bitter Winter's day ~ just awful in terms of weather.

The feeling of planting a legacy like this will stay with me for all time. Some humans don't plant a single tree in their lifetime. Others spend their whole lives planting trees. We no longer have the land upon which those trees are planted, but we do visit occasionally and watch and marvel at their growth, and how beautifully they're maturing. Soon we'll be moving across the country, and won't get to see the orchard again. Like life, we don't always see the fruition of our work, but it's no less meaningful. The work and play of our children's lives are meaningful, whether we get to witness the fruit and harvest of them or not ~ sometimes it can take decades to see the 'results'. Allowing our children freedom to follow their own loves and interests is the most empowering gift a parent can bestow upon their child. This can be viewed with clarity when we've wiped the muck of cultural conditioning from our spectacles!

As unschoolers, we offer our children their whole childhood to play, to discover what sets their hearts alight and brings laughter to their souls.

Do What You Love

If there's only one message I hope my children take from childhood, it's this: *do what you love.* As a parent, I'm happy to support them for however long it takes to reach this point. Somehow, though, I think they'll discover this far earlier in life than I did.

Our society expects children to know what they want to do with their *whole life* before they've reached adulthood. For some humans, this comes easily and with great clarity. For others, life has to be fully explored for many years before there's an 'aha' moment. As unschoolers, we offer our children their whole childhood to play, to discover what sets their hearts alight and brings laughter to their souls. At this moment, my girls are showing areas they're drawn to. For Bethany, this includes music, writing, composing, fashion design and psychology. For Eliza, it's the culinary arts (including photography), music, writing, history and theatre. They've also had opportunities, and still do, to experience many other fields.

In my last year of secondary school, I did work experience at The Children's Cottage, a beautiful Montessori school. My form teacher must have had good feedback, as the reference she wrote me after school included high praise for my work with children. I later ended up working with children in one form or another (another Montessori school, a childcare centre, nannying, a Steiner school, a professional babysitting agency), and later on, in the media ~ writing. It wasn't until my mid thirties that I connected both these areas together, and began publishing The Mother magazine ~ a passionate contribution to the world, dedicated to raising children with awareness. I simply couldn't have done this work at 16, or even at 26, as I didn't have the experience: personally, practically or spiritually. Sometimes life has to grow on you, and through experience you discover your strengths and passions. You find your feet. Don't we owe it to our children to give them the freedom to find their own feet, rather than force them into 'acceptable' shoes? I trust that my children will journey through life, as I have, always committed to working in jobs, and with people, that they love. I never stayed in a job for money, and indeed, most of my jobs have been pitifully paid. Interestingly, I'm also learning that I can do what I love and not be broke! My girls are learning the value of doing what they love, and honouring what they do, and who they are.

Salsa dancing, illustrated by Bethany

Salsa Sisters

Bethany and Eliza have two older sisters, Hannah and Harriet, who live in New Zealand. Given we left New Zealand in 1998, it had been a long time since our last meeting. Bethany was two and a half, and Eliza six months.

When their eldest sister, Hannah came to visit a couple of years ago, I was so grateful that the girls weren't in school. It meant they had two weeks of full-on sister time, and learnt salsa dancing from Hannah. She's fluent in Spanish, Mandarin, and Portugese. Hannah's also well-travelled, and has lived in Latin America and China. She was able to share many stories with her little sisters, about people in indigenous cultures. In turn, they showed her the wonders of knitting and baking bread; skills of the Slow Movement. They were able to touch each other's lives uninterrupted by institutional education. Had they been at school, they'd have had to ask permission from the principal for two weeks off. This would most certainly have been declined because it would have been seen as detrimental to their education.

Parents are at the mercy of the 'authority' within their children's institution of learning.

Their other sister, Harriet, 29, has just visited us en route from Ireland, where she'd been visiting her boyfriend's family. Again, I found myself giving thanks that we're not part of a system which interferes with family life.

I have to ask, though, why people think it's acceptable to be dictated to like this. Why do they tolerate such abuse and violation of basic liberties? Perhaps it's just so ingrained, like having to ask permission to empty your bowel or bladder, or being told when you're allowed to eat, rather than eating when you're hungry. There's a craziness to our society, and this is manifested so clearly in the school system.

Harriet, Hannah, Bethany and Eliza, in Auckland, New Zealand 1998

The Unschoolers Go To School

Spring, 2004 ~ The Mother magazine, Issue Nine

The UK government has been having a bit of a rant lately about the bad parents who take their children on holidays inside school term time. Heaven forbid! We wouldn't want anyone enjoying un-interrupted family life now, would we?

Of course we can see through the spin. It's just another little plot to keep parents under control; another scheme to dis-empower people at their vulnerable centre. After all, despite how much time we spend trying to impress others with jobs, letters after our name, five cars, or whatever, nothing, but nothing, gives us a true mirror of who we are, and of our own evolution, in quite the same way as our family does. And strangely enough, even though most politicians find this hard to believe, many families do want to spend time together. They want family time which doesn't involve the routine of jobs and school. So it was with joyous heart that Paul and I set off with our unschooled bambini to Italy during 'school term time'.

Our visit included spending the afternoon in an English language class for young children, at the school attended by the children of a friend of ours.

I found the experience a good reminder of my time in classrooms, and how hard it is for little kids to sit still and concentrate. Also, why it takes so long to teach children anything when they're learning a forced curriculum with many other children. It certainly made me reflect on the non-stop questioning which happens in an unschooling environment, and how that need simply can't be met with so many children to teach in a classroom.

After leaving Rimini, we travelled north to the Emilio-Romagna region, north of Umbria. From our beloved Pennines in the UK, to the Apennines in Italy.

We stayed in a Fattoria (Italian Farmhouse) on an organic orchard and vineyard, where they grow cherries, apricots, plums, persimmons and an assortment of vegetables for the local box scheme. Agricultural tourism is becoming very popular in Italy.

Claudio, the owner of the orchard, left his hectic life as a world-travelling cardiologist, to live the quiet life. His Summer sounded anything but quiet to me. Daily, he has groups of about 30 school children come to the orchard; and they bake bread, collect honey, make scarecrows, and learn about fruit production. We had the pleasure to see newborn kids (tiny Tibetan goats) just half an hour old. We delighted in all the farm animals, each with a name and a life, and not destined for the dinner table.

On a hillside, Claudio showed us a wall of sediment which has various layers of soil, sand and stone from the past two million years. Thirty years ago, a complete whale skeleton was found on adjacent land. This area used to be an ocean.

In terms of education, my children were gifted with many things during that trip. Subjects were interwoven, as is life, such as archaeology, languages, culture, animal husbandry (we watched mama goat eat the placenta), horticulture, maths (working in Euros rather than pounds), humanity (the illegal immigrants who begged for money in the car parks. One of them didn't quite know what to make of the bananas I gave him), transport, communication, and friendships where there's no common language spoken.

Life on the land, Spring, 2004: back at home in England, Spring is here. Daffodils, crocuses, and mini irises are parading the land. The late February snow has lain a blanket of thick white across the four acre field. How many animals have crossed it has been quickly revealed by an assortment of footprints. There are some we've yet to identify.

Bethany's been helping me create a huge spiral herb garden. It's been a fun way to learn about circumferences (walking around in Bethany-sized steps), and *experiencing* a diameter and radius. This real study of circles is more easily understood this way, especially for a visual child like Bethany.

Someone asked me recently what it is that I prefer about unschooling to a classroom. There are many reasons, of course, but something that occurred the other day was a good example.

Bethany loves making books. She'll spend hours, days even, on writing a story, and illustrating it in great detail. She plans to publish all her books one day.

She'd been sitting on her swing beneath the crab apple tree on our land, writing her story for some time. I was preparing a vegetable bed. When she'd had enough, Bethany brought the book to my wheelbarrow for me to look after while she went and played. It's this setting and timing of their own learning that resonates with unschoolers. She seamlessly let go of all the energy she'd been invest-

*They don't have to try and concentrate
on learning something
when their body is telling them it needs fuel.*

ing into the day's creation of her book, and then jumped on top of a huge straw bale to play with her sister.

The next hour was spent laughing, playing with water, and watering the new willow tunnel and hedge that will shelter the beehives. The girls choose when to eat their snacks. They don't have to try and concentrate on learning something when their body's telling them it needs fuel. To me, school is alien to what children need, although I'm not saying that there aren't good schools, or indeed brilliant teachers.

Another aspect of unschooling is having your children around a lot more than the average parent. It's very easy on a bad day to think that sending your children to school will fix things up. I'm not the first unschooler or homeschooler to have had *that* thought. The truth is, though, that the issue is about family dynamics. School can act as a bandaid to family dysfunction, but that is all it can do. It will never heal a relationship; will never create an opportunity to develop closeness between a parent and child if there are issues to address.

We all have things that press our buttons. Removing challenging children from the bulk of our daylight hours does not, and never will, remove those annoying buttons we possess. They're *our* buttons, not theirs. Our children are playing the wonderful role of healer by showing us the things we need to look at within ourselves. By removing children from our day-to-day life, we simply make space for other people to come along and do their 'button pressing' job. Our children, without question, are our greatest teachers.

*Choosing
to remove children
from school,
or not sending them there
in the first place,
means looking at the
wound,
and possibly
picking at the scab!*

Healing The Wound

*"Don't worry Mary. I'll bet Pa would still love us
if neither of us got an A."*
Laura to her sister, Mary, Little House on the Prairie.

Choosing to home educate or unschool your child or children will almost certainly bring up your own feelings about school when you were growing up. There's no question that we're shaped by our early life, and when school forms such a huge part of that ~ on average ten to 13 years of life ~ our views will be coloured one way or another. For some parents, even if their school days were painful or difficult, they've come away with a belief that 'school toughens you up for the real world', and that that must be a good thing. It's so common to hear 'it never did me any harm', and yet, if you can engage such people in conversation, as I often do, and really help them to explore their feelings honestly, you'll soon discover that they harbour a lot of pain, and that school, in their case, did do them some harm.

Often it feels safer to leave our wounds well-covered. Choosing to remove children from school, or not sending them there in the first place, means looking at the wound, and possibly picking at the scab!

Why were we so badly hurt? Was it something personal about us? Were we a round peg in a square hole? What made us so different? Why weren't our needs catered for? The wound reveals the cure!

After overcoming initial fears of whether we're capable enough of teaching our children (especially, if, like me, you failed some subjects at school!), we soon realise that unschooling isn't a case of 'us and them'. This is a voyage that the *whole family* is on, and I doubt there's a family around where the parents know the answers to every question that will ever be asked.

We're all learning, and when, as an adult, we take that on board and step away from our role as the authoritarian in the learning relationship, we soon see how much fun it is to learn together, or individually, and then come back together to share our findings. The day we honour our children is the day we begin to heal.

We are 'high touch' creatures
(when living naturally).
I don't believe school fulfills the needs
we have as humans
because we're not encouraged
to touch, hug and comfort
when in the school environment.
We're taught to compete.

The Sociable Child

There's an amusing cartoon which shows the myth and reality of socialisation. The myth is that school socialises children, and the reality is kids are forced together like sardines in a can.

I also laugh at another cartoon which shows children at the bus stop. The signpost says ~ school to the right, and beach to the left. The home educated children are heading to the beach!

All children are social. It's our perception of what social means that needs examining, and so does the way in which humans socialise. Some people thrive in large groups, and need people around them all the time. Others prefer one on one interactions, and plenty of time to themselves. Every human being is different. For example, I really enjoy having a few friends over to dinner. When one particular friend phones me and says, "Hey, come and have some dinner with us", I KNOW that it won't be just the two of us, but all her dozens of friends will be there, and she'll be hosting a party. That's how she socialises. I prefer more intimate dinners.

My husband and I are what might be termed, in personality profiling, as extroverts. It's true that we can engage people easily, friends or strangers, and that our first response to meeting someone is almost always to smile and be welcoming. It's not true that we have parties all the time and need people around us 24/7. I, for one, love (and need) solitude.

One of my daughters goes out into the world with a 'shy' face. That is, most people who don't know her well would see her as shy, and if they knew she was home educated would almost certainly say that that's why she's shy. If we put her in school, they suggest, she'd overcome her shyness. I wonder why that didn't work for all my adult friends who are both shy *and* attended school for 12 plus years? My daughter, incidentally, rules the roost any time she's comfortable and familiar in a setting. As a family, we don't see her as shy.

Through my study of psychological astrology, I've learnt to understand humans, and human relationships, so much better. Had I not learned what I know now, I may well have come to believe that school would make my daughter less shy, and maybe even 'outgoing', like her parents! I'm not going to pretend that my children have loads of friends and that socialisation has never been an issue. It has. But I can, hand on heart, say that the biggest issue hasn't been because the girls have been, primarily, home educated, but because we live rurally, and that the nature of most of the people who live in our area is vastly different to ours, and to the lifestyle we live, as a family. It can be immensely challenging for other people when your children don't eat junk food, drink Coke, nor own a mobile phone, or play with plastic toys, eat a botanical diet, etc. All this, when thrown into a subculture of people with few expansive social skills makes it difficult to form friendships.

As Paul and I have become older, we've also found ourselves less likely to form relationships with people for the sake of it, but rather, have saved our energy for those of like mind. I would love to have waved a wand and gifted my daughters with lovely friends to play with. They do have friends, but the children they love don't live close by.

As humans, we don't tend to live in isolation, but in company. We are 'high touch' creatures (when living naturally). I don't believe school fulfills the needs we have as humans because we're not encouraged to touch, hug and comfort when in the school environment. We're taught to compete. It's a war. It's survival of the fittest, not of the most loving, caring, compassionate or forgiving. The culture is based on blame.

I was bullied throughout school and into early adulthood. No one bullies me now, regardless of who they are or what position they're in. Did school make me a better person by 'toughening' me up? NO. If I'd been raised without all the torment, I'd have found my soul blossoming; and, with my roots strong and secure, I'd not have attracted such nasty people into my life over and over again. I'd also be more likely to have attained the peace levels of a dove.

It's been my desire that our children have a strong sense of self, and attract warm, loving and kind people into their world. School certainly showed them the other side! Ironically, her chief bully in secondary school, ended up sharing the daily twenty minute taxi ride with Bethany. We've explained to the girls that sometimes people turn up in our lives to show us parts of ourselves that we might call our 'shadow self' ~ the murkier side, which we tend to deny. From a homeopathic standpoint of 'like attracts like', we ask ourselves why a nasty, bossy or rude person shows up in our life. We ask: what are they showing me about myself? What needs healing within my psyche?

Child-led Learning

In 2006, I became a bit like a sunflower ~ noticeable to all in the garden! The only thing was, the garden was pretty huge and covered the whole planet. And, it seems, not everyone likes sunflowers!

My family and I appeared on a programme called Extraordinary Breastfeeding. It was initially shown on Channel Four in the UK, but has since been seen all around the world, and extracts also used for other documentaries.

Viewed by dozens of millions of people, the documentary asked: at what age should a baby/child wean? We answered honestly, and readily opened up our family life to the public gaze. My main message was this: children wean when they're ready. Even within the breastfeeding and natural parenting world there was outrage that I could suggest it be 'natural' for a child to be breastfeeding at seven years of age ~ as my children were. The medical, anthropological and biological evidence supports full-term breastfeeding. The only reason that a child wouldn't breastfeed until their milk teeth came out, is *cultural*. That is, because you, I or someone else decides it's unacceptable. And our children's health, well-being and psychological stability are based on someone's opinion?

My daughters weaned when they'd had enough. My part of the breastfeeding experience meant learning that breastfeeding isn't just about milk and nutrition, but that the psychological benefits of affectionate bonding and mother love go hand in hand.

The vast majority of people cast me out, and labelled me a freak, paedophile and possessive mother. The world didn't understand that I wasn't just comforting my children (which anyone can do), I was *nurturing* them.

Child-led weaning is like child-led learning: we trust that our baby/child will tell us what she needs. A breastfed baby will create all the milk that's needed, and in the right nutritional proportions for his or her age and stage; and an unschooled child will ensure he or she receives the learning that's needed for their unique path through life. After all, it's THEIR life, and they have an investment in their future in a way that *no one else truly has, not even their parents*. A child, when left to discover their passions, *will* find them.

*The angst, stress, anxiety and pressure
to perform, mark these years ~
a time when our body is begging us to play.*

Bethany at 13, out for a walk just out of the village.

Teens and Unschooling

"...one who learns from life and love and great books and late-morning conversations and big projects and eccentric uncles and mountains and mistakes and volunteering and starry nights ~ not from dull textbooks and sedative lectures and interfering homework." Definition of unschooler, by Grace Llewellyn, author of The Teenage Liberation Handbook.

Do you remember your teenage years? All those mood swings, all those hormones? Did you feel as if no-one understood you? Perhaps you felt you were born into the wrong family?

Teens rarely feel that they have any sense of control over their lives. Our body, at that age, is dictating our direction with hormones which tell us one thing, while our culture tells us another. They're diametrically opposed messages.

At school, academic achievement is the priority ~ as it prepares teenagers to go out into the world. The angst, stress, anxiety and pressure to perform, mark these years ~ a time when our body is begging us to play. The play may be different to that of early childhood, but it's equally valid. This play will take different forms, depending on the child concerned, but largely it's meant to be for discovering our magical self, and our emerging sexuality. This comes through creativity, fun and friendships, not the stress of exams.

This culture has a fear of sexuality, and seeks to debase it at every level. The emergence of this part of our selves during our teenage years is a picture of how our creativity can develop. Sexual energy is *creative* energy. How do we use that energy? Is it expressed by sitting at a desk trying to regurgitate information on a set curriculum?

Unschooling offers freedom from culture's messages, especially for teenagers. In this space, the young adult can explore their emotions more readily, through a channel that feels right for them ~ such as drama or writing or design. The channelling of such energy can last for hours and hours, if not days or weeks, and is not limited to a half hour slot abruptly aborted by a bell.

The school system survives because of a pecking order.
If you step out of line, you'll be pecked,
prodded and pushed until you get back into line.
Rebelliousness and authenticity
are not encouraged.

A flower for Mum, by Eliza, aged nine.

The Rhythm of Family Life

A school can only function using routine. It's impossible to recreate home in a school room, because of the unnatural situation of grouping so many children together (and usually of the same age) with only one or two adults.

School is based on a set programme of 'learning', which must be achieved in a set time. In order for this to happen, a strict routine is put into place. Children's young lives then follow this routine. Their bodily functions must accord with an external monitor that tells them when they can wee, poo, eat, drink, play, daydream, make friends, and rest. These natural processes must fit in around the more important elements of 'learning'. There's no room for intimacy, or the expression of genuine emotion. The school system survives because of a pecking order. If you step out of line, you'll be pecked, prodded and pushed until you get back into line. Rebelliousness and authenticity are not encouraged.

At home, when unschooling, bodily functions take priority. Whether we need to laugh, cry, eat, sleep, go to the loo, play or have a glass of water, we can do so freely, without anyone's permission. The day is based on a gentle rhythm. Learning always occurs, and is therefore never forced into a box. A child's learning happens because we, as adults, get out of the way.

Cat mask, by Bethany at aged six.

Bethany's painting of Nun in the Sunset, when she was aged ten.

100% Responsibility

Someone once asked me if home education was a 'middle class' thing. Raised in Australia, 'class' is anathema to me. That aside, choosing human-scale education is about consciousness, not class. As much as anything, I'd like my girls to bring consciousness to all that they do, and to who they are.

When looking at my philosophical questions about unschooling and how children learn, I come back, time and time again, to wanting my daughters to understand that they're 100% responsible for their lives. Obviously, I need to lead by example. This hasn't always been easy for me. One of the stories in this book is a testament to that. I spent four years grieving about the land we sold because of a court case. A lifetime dream seemingly snatched from my hands. I was riddled with anger, guilt (should I have made other decisions, such as letting the farmer bully me, rather than standing my ground?), feeling like a victim, and full of blame. Although, in some cases, time does heal, what usually happens with time is that our perspective changes. When the hot and angry boil isn't being squeezed, and has had time for the toxins to dissolve, we can see things without blinkers on, and pain masking the truth.

I believe that every person who walks this planet is responsible for their life. They're responsible, whether they like it/admit it, or not; and the sooner we learn to take responsibility for everything that happens in our life, and more importantly, our *reaction* to it, the more accepting of our life's path we'll be.

Humans are made of about 80% water, and as high water creatures, we're very connected to everything within the 'field' around us. Every time we have a thought or belief, this is amplified into the world. I'm sure you can think of someone you know who's always attracting bad luck or dramas. It's as if it's drawn to them. It is! We draw *everything* into our life: the good, the bad and the ugly. How we draw them in is based on what information is stored in our subconscious. We can say all the affirmations in the world, and introduce new ideas to our conscious mind, but if we've got a library full of internal information to the contrary, we'll keep on attracting more of the same.

One of the tools I'm using to help me let go of all false memories is that of Ho'oponopono, an ancient Hawaiian teaching. In many ways, this is like a daily meditation. It doesn't require sitting down in a quiet room for twenty minutes, but is done every time a memory comes up. The interesting thing I've found is that once you start this process, you begin to remember all sorts of past hurts, grievances, etc. They seem to fly from all reaches of the Universe. I often find myself thinking, "Did I really 'hang on' to that?" We hang on to everything, until we choose to release it. This might seem intimidating, and a very good reason not to even start on such a process, but it's infinitely nicer (and kinder to mind, body and soul) to be free of resentments, anger, fear and vengeance. We often think we're in control of our lives, but if we have hundreds and thousands more subconscious thoughts (like a CD quietly playing in the background) than conscious ones, we can't know if our plans, goals and best intentions are being sabotaged. No one can remove these false limitations but ourselves.

My girls are using Ho'oponopono in their lives, whether it's about difficulties they have with learning a musical piece, a disagreement they have with each other, friendships, a cough, visiting the dentist or music exam nerves.

I don't believe life has to be difficult, but that we can all grow through love, joy, laughter and fun. We can't get there though if we live with blame, shame, guilt, fear and distrust. Schools are sub-cultures of the larger culture, and are based on blame and adversarial relationships.

"The purpose of life is to be restored back to Love, moment to moment.
To fulfil this purpose, the individual must acknowledge
that he is 100 percent responsible for creating his life the way it is.
He must come to see that it is his thoughts that create his life the way it is
moment to moment.
The problems are not people, places and situations,
but rather the thoughts of them.
He must come to appreciate that there is no such thing as 'out there'.

~ Dr. Ihaleakala Hew Len.

Life with School

A friend had given Bethany a copy of Harry Potter in 2005. She read all the available books in the series avidly. Wow, if schools were like Hogwarts, what an amazing place to be! Magic makes the world go round.

By February 2007, she was asking to go to school. It went against everything I believed and understood about how children learn. I was tortured. However, I also believe that it's vital to trust our children, and if she was hearing 'the call' to go to school, then I had to put my beliefs and thoughts out of the way. It wasn't easy. The wake up call came after the dream. Actually, it was a nightmare. A mother's worst nightmare… I dreamt that Bethany was sleeping, but running out of oxygen. There was a small candle near her face, but it was stealing all the air from her room. I woke with a start. I knew immediately that the oxygen she needed was a change of environment.

Bethany had been Eliza's constant companion for nine years, so when Bethany and I drove to school to enrol her, Eliza stayed in the car feeling rather forlorn. When Bethany and I came back to the car to say she was starting in two weeks (after the half term break), Eliza said she'd go to school, too. Eliza had had no intentions of going, but it was clear that she didn't want to be left at home all day without her sister.

Their months at school, from March to October, were a time of much 'biting my tongue'. The puncture marks lasted a long time. I no longer wrote my column in The Mother about unschooling, but my editorials from that time tell the story of our family's journey.

Holding On, Letting Go

May/June, 2007 ~ The Mother magazine, Issue 22

I'm currently going through a rather life-changing experience of letting go; not just of my daughters, or a way of life, but of a set of beliefs.

The process is very much like that of going through the stages of grief. I look to Mother Nature, always my guru, to see what I can learn from this emotionally difficult time.

When we co-create with our partner to conceive a much longed for baby, we hold on to each other and the wish for conception. In a place of trust, we have no alternative but to let go.

The sperm meets the egg, and together, they hold on. And then, a letting go must happen for the embryo to travel up the fallopian tube.

Our body holds tight to the placenta, and we let go of it at birth. Already our parenting is taking on a pattern: an eternal breath of inhale, exhale.

Our baby arrives, and if our intuitive mothering is intact, we hold on. We might even hold on for six or so months, like Balinese women, before putting our child down to touch the ground. Eventually though, we let go, so our baby can feel the ground, and learn to crawl. They'll crawl away from us.

Our parenting path is based on these two diametrically opposed acts: holding on and letting go. Somehow the holding on doesn't create the same dramas in our life. Yet both experiences are equally valid, and entirely necessary for evolution. If we don't grow, don't blossom, we eat into ourselves, and die.

As a passionate advocate for child-led, human-scale education, our family way of living was rocked to the core by my daughters' decision to 'try out school'. Living rurally has impacted on the availability of friendships for them. They do have friends, but not nearly as many as they'd like.

How in my heart could I reconcile everything I understand about how children learn, with them deliberately placing themselves in an educational setting far removed from my ideals? To say I was challenged doesn't even come close to how I felt, and still feel.

What I've learnt over the years is that the greatest gift we can give our children is that of trust. And trust, I have.

Each day that my children climb aboard the school bus, I trust they'll experience the day in a way which opens their mind, heart and soul. I trust that their teachers recognise them as humans, rather than as numbers on a government supplied statistic sheet.

As I write, just five weeks into their school experience, they've both made comments about choosing home education for secondary school. For Bethany, that means this September, which is rather ironic, because her desire to try out primary school was to give her some school experience before entering high school.

My experience of the girls being in mainstream education includes the shocking realisation that the 'system' isn't something I can change or control in any way, at least not on my own. That the school actually doesn't want input from parents, or to be told how to educate, is restrictive, to say the least. Ok, I knew this already, but you can't blame a mum for trying!

Mainstream education needs a radical overhaul. These changes won't come from above. The government has targets to meet, and that is its concern. Our concern, as parents, goes far deeper, and it's from here that we can act. If... if we act together. It simply shouldn't be acceptable to have 20+ children piled into one classroom. How can they possibly have their needs met this way?

What sort of culture do we live in where you have to buy education if you don't like what's on offer for the masses? Why is it that home educators don't get tax reductions, given they're not using the resources their taxes go towards? Why can't governments fund alternative schools? The money is still allocated for your child, so why should the government determine which school your child should go to in order to get the benefits of YOUR tax money? Why isn't anyone speaking up about this? Why are we such an apathetic nation?

There are so many reasons why I don't want my children in school, and I simply can't see how the benefit of a few extra friends can possibly outweigh the deleterious effects of a factory farm approach to education.

My daughters, known for their love of food, have cut their daily food consumption in half because they don't get "enough time" to eat at morning and afternoon break; and most importantly, for them, there's nowhere to sit down and eat! This contravenes the very nature of our digestive process ~ the need to be in a state of relaxation. Children are encouraged to run around while they eat an apple ~ ironic with the health and safety red tape which strangles the system. Most days, in amongst the fun elements of school, the girls complain about how much time is wasted by the teacher yelling at the disruptive pupils. I try and explain that these children are seeking attention, most likely because they don't get it at home from their parents. The chances are they'll spend their waking hours at home glued to a TV or computer screen.

I've been horrified at how much time at school is spent by children playing computer games and watching DVDs ~ all under the fancy title of media studies or ICT (information computer technology). Who are they trying to kid? What does my daughter get out of a computer game? Call me cynical, but I feel this use of televisual stimulus is nothing more than a band-aid: an acceptable childminder in a school culture that simply can't meet the needs of 25 plus children at once. Bethany's class was due to watch a horror film ~ but FORTUNATELY the TV didn't work! She wouldn't be watching that sort of show at home, so what right do the teachers have to inflict violence on them at school?

Bethany is in year six: a few short months till secondary school. When she came home with her spelling list, and the word 'perfectionist' was spelt wrong, I 'tsk tskd'. 'Fancy allowing a typo on a 'spelling list' to go unnoticed', I thought. At least, I assumed it was a typo. The next day, Bethany mentioned the 'typo' to the teacher, who had to look it up in the dictionary: and then told the children to add an 'i' to the word when they got home!

At present, I've 'let go' of the need to keep my children out of regimented, institutional learning. They know that the option to be home educated again is always there. And likewise, if we move towards a position of living in an area with an appropriate, affordable, human-scale school, they can try that, too.

For now, I trust that my children will be able to retain their free spirit, that they won't sink under the weight of the school's control, and that they'll always fly. I see their independent thinking blossoming amidst ideas we, in our family, find odd. When Bethany had an assignment to draw God, she knew that you couldn't put the infinite into the finite. And perhaps it is, too, with my children, that their souls will never be suppressed in this culture; that they've touched freedom for enough of their childhood not to be drawn into the myth of what most people consider to be education.

As for me, after the initial adjustment, this has come to feel like a well-earned break after 11 years of full-time parenting. My days are filled with writing a book, walking, editing The Mother, and gardening. I do believe that the Western world is waking up to realise that less is more; that a life well lived isn't one of accumulation, but of what we give away: not of what we hold on to, but of what we let go.

Why Am I So Ugly?
July/August, 2007 ~ The Mother magazine, Issue 23

When I was in secondary school, I learnt not to eat breakfast. Who has time for breakfast when you've a date with the mirror each morning? My mother would squeeze me a fresh orange juice so I had something in my tummy, but I certainly didn't have time to sit down and eat. This habit has stayed with me throughout adulthood. Eating breakfast isn't something which comes naturally to me.

Now that my girls are in school, I can't believe how much time they spend in front of the mirror in the mornings. We never had this before, when they were home-educated. Mirrors were for parading in front of with full dressing-up attire, not for examining facial features, and brushing hair one hundred times.

Eliza's been asking me a lot lately, "Why am I so ugly?" I don't know if there are many other words that could break a mother's heart so easily. Throughout my pregnancies, and from the day both girls were born, I told them how beautiful they were. Both Paul and I always affirmed their beauty, physical and spiritual, and honoured them for who they are, not what they do.

All these years of affirmations are being eroded by other voices. Both girls love school, and yet insidious elements are creeping into our lives on a daily basis. I find myself breathing deeply, counting to ten, and then throwing my hands up to the gods in exasperation, saying "Now what?" I often feel like I'm in uncharted waters, completely at a loss as to how to affirm my daughters when the 'world' is giving them contrary messages. As parents, we feel like we're a lone voice in the wilderness.

The messages the world gives me, as a mother, are along the lines of "It'll toughen 'em up for the real world when they're adults." I always wonder what pain people are hiding when they regurgitate *that* myth. Who are they trying to convince?

In my garden I find that if seedlings and saplings are nurtured, nourished and accommodated according to their biological needs, they'll grow and flourish ~ their blueprint is to *thrive*. If I was to provide hostile conditions in their growing environment, they might still grow, but they certainly wouldn't thrive as is their true nature. Common sense dictates that this is no way to raise seedlings.

What makes people think our children, as living creatures, are any different in design? How can crushing their souls toughen them up? My soul and being were knocked 'into shape' through childhood bullying and insensitive teachers, and I can say without doubt, that it hasn't prepared me for the real world; hasn't made me a better person. It *never* has a positive influence on our personal evolution, and to suggest otherwise is ignorance of what it means to be divine beings.

Every adult I know who was bullied at school is emphatic that the wounds are still there within them, and they're not the person they could have been, as a result. Achieving our potential, and being inspired to reach for the optimum, comes through nurturing, not torture and tyranny.

It's nothing more than a collective duping, a dumbing down, that has us believing that toughening kids up is a good thing. Of course, no one likes to be challenged on such core beliefs, as it threatens their whole way of being and living. It's far easier to live like sheep than to step aside and question cultural norms.

So, while my daughter questions her physical appearance and her emerging personality, based on jibes from school children, I wonder when she'll start doubting her *inner* beauty and strength, too.

When I questioned her as to why she hadn't shared with me, or a teacher, about one persistent bully, she replied that "The children lie, and say they didn't do anything, so there's no point in telling a teacher, because it makes me look like a liar."

Is this where we learn to hide our truth? Does authenticity die when we don't see it mirrored in the lives of those who inhabit our environment? Do we retreat into our deepest, innermost self, and then shrivel away? I know that as Eliza looks in the mirror each morning, she's trying to see herself whole again ~ trying to recapture what I've always told her, rather than the broken mirror image held up to her each day by her peers.

Both my girls are of an age where they desire to grow away from me. This is natural ~ another milestone in our family's journey.

On my wedding day, in my late twenties, my mother revealed that she could finally stop worrying about me. I was shocked. I'd left home as an independent sixteen year old. What had she been worrying about? And, now I'm a mother, with a different perspective, I'll bet she still worries about me when my life isn't going smoothly. We may stop carrying our children on our hips, but we always carry them in our hearts.

As for my daughters, I want them to grow up and fully embrace the world, just as I have. My goal is not to protect them from life, as many people seem to fear. Rather, it's to have them emerge from childhood as strong, secure and well-loved as possible. The greater our self-love, the richer our experiences of love and life.

As parents, we need to remind our children to come back to themselves; to close their eyes and feel their beauty, strength and spirit. That coming back into themselves, and listening to their own song, is the best validation they'll ever have of their own beauty.

I know women ~ *gorgeous* women ~ who were given such negative messages about themselves as children. Maybe their hair was too red and curly, or they got an A instead of an A+ in their school report. Some women had too many freckles, or skinny arms; others were more artistically orientated than mathematical, which led to parental disappointment. I can't imagine how a parent could imprint such prejudice upon their child, yet it happens the world over.

"You talk too much", "You should have been a boy", "I hate your hair colour". "I don't know how you ended up in this family, you're not like us!" "I wish you were more like your sister".

Recently, a lunchtime supervisor at my daughters' school was reported to have said to one young student, "No wonder your mother hates you!" How on Earth does a child become more of who they are with such invalidation?

Parenting is always about leading by example. All of us can be a living vision of what self-love in action looks like. It begins with self-appreciation, and loving everything about yourself. *The Breathmaker* created us all beautiful. Sadly, this isn't on the National Curriculum.

Every time we look outside ourselves for validation or sense of self, through clothes, make-up, material possessions, companions, etc., we're not able to see who we really are.

Those who don't see our beauty haven't seen it within themselves. Walk in beauty today, knowing that it's impossible, by nature of your divine heritage, for you to be anything else.

Cuddles are Compulsory

Nov/Dec, 2007 ~ The Mother magazine, Issue 25

My girls have decided to leave school, and return to home education. The past eight months have been an interesting and sobering journey, both for me as a mother, but also for us, as a family. The silence in the home has felt like a fabricated, if not superficial, peace. For me, each day they were at school held an undercurrent of angst. I imagined my daughters in a loveless school room, being taught things which, for the most part, were totally irrelevant to healthy, vibrant, conscious living, and at odds with our family's vision of life.

The decision to opt for home education again has come from them, not me or their Dad, though clearly the whole family has been involved in various discussions and considerations.

This past term for Eliza has been based on a curriculum of learning about World War 2. The UK government clearly thinks it's important for nine year olds to have their days filled with images and stories of gas masks and concentration camps. As a family, we don't focus on war, but look at how humans can live in peace, within their own mind, and, also, within the world.

Bethany made a loaf of bread in school earlier in the year. This involved weeks of work, writing and designing the loaf of bread, and umpteen other bits of curriculum-related written work ~ all in order to satisfy a government check-list. In real life, you just get on and make a loaf of bread. In our family, the main requirement for bread making is for the baker to be in a good mood, so she can 'grow' the dough with love. That's not technical or scientific enough to make it onto the National Curriculum.

In secondary school, Bethany's class was taught how to 'cut an apple' (yes, you read that right!). It begs the question: "what's happening in homes up and down the country that the government believes children of eleven and twelve years of age need a lesson in apple cutting?" The curriculum also includes how to make a sandwich. Bethany's sandwich of Brazil nut and linseed rye bread, filled with hommous, grated carrot, cucumber and rocket, was completely out of place in a room of white bread sandwiches filled with chocolate spread. My children have been using these very basic skills for many years.

The UK Prime Minister, Gordon Brown, is seeking to create world class schools in the UK. It's very admirable; however, he'd do well to actually spend some extended time in a school room, experiencing it through the eyes and heart of a child, and then he might see where the improvements need to be made.

Like the children, I suspect many teachers have had their humanity squashed out of them in order to survive in the system. A loving respect for children seems largely missing, as does an awareness of holistic child development, and health and well-being. I'm ever so glad my girls were nine and 11 before they tried out school. This gave them enough awareness and understanding of life and consensus reality to see through a number of issues.

When they started school in March, both girls bounced out of bed in the mornings with excitement; they jumped off the school bus in the afternoons itching to tell me all about their day. They couldn't tell me quickly enough about everything they'd done. I started to question if I'd been wrong to home educate them for so long.

As the weeks turned into months, the sparkle started disappearing from their eyes. The end of day reports were narrowed down to 'didn't do anything in school today', or 'science was boring', or 'the teacher spent the whole time yelling at the naughty boys'. The bouncing out of bed at 6am became: "Eliza, it's eight o'clock, time to get up, there's only half an hour left till the bus is here." It's not surprising that she'd had enough. I certainly wouldn't enjoy spending six hours a day listening to someone yelling. What a stressful environment. No wonder she came home with headaches.

For Bethany, entering secondary school has turned out to be far different from the idealised image portrayed in Harry Potter and the Jacqueline Wilson books! She's quickly come to question why she should only be allowed one art and one music lesson a week, when they're clearly her favourite subjects and in the direction of what she believes to be her life's purpose. "Why should I learn algebra?" (My sentiments exactly, honey!). "What's that got to do with being an artist?" When she started school, we helped her along by having some weekly maths tutoring. This option, to help her learn maths, will be revisited as and when she desires. At the moment, she needs to detox from "I hate Mondays, we've got maths." The Prime Minister wants to increase the number of hours a week that children do physical education ~ not a bad thing at all, but at Bethany's former school that means subjects like art will be sacrificed to make time for it. One of the drawcards for attending school was to develop friendships. The reality is, there's very little time for playing and socialising in school. They both plan to see their school friends after school and at weekends, and rejoin the local Education Otherwise (home ed) group, as well as joining other groups.

It's a blissfully sunny Autumn afternoon, and the girls are in the back garden playing with three children from the village. This play time can go on for hours, and isn't dictated by a bell, and having to gulp down lunch in order to grab a few minutes of play.

A friend of mine always says, "If it ain't fun, I ain't doin' it!" Lest I forget, this quote is on my vision board, and the girls have adopted it as their home education motto. This is clearly seen in their delightful and carefully thought out personal curriculum.

Watching the girls make plans for an individualised map of learning has been fascinating, and an absolute joy. A few times, I've caught my breath at the sheer delight and empowerment they're experiencing in choosing their learning path. Eliza and Bethany love to learn. They thoroughly enjoy doing projects and being immersed in activities. They've come to realise though, that this time is better spent planning their own learning than having it, or their time, dictated to them. Bethany's class was given mass punishment because of two disruptive pupils. "Why should I give up my lunch break if I didn't do anything wrong?" Is this how our schools teach justice and fairness?

Home-based learning allows a child to trust in his/her ability to find a path of learning which reflects their uniqueness, creativity, interest, curiosity and spontaneity. Our job, as parents, whether we home educate or not, is to offer a rich environment so that the child will easily find what she needs in order to learn. If a child desires to learn, then she'll enthusiastically absorb that information. This is the opposite of the rote learning and memorisation of subjects which occur in schools. Our culture appears to be unaware of the impact of imposing education upon children.

If Gordon Brown really wants to create world class education, he needs to understand that it's a far greater skill to ask questions than to know the answers to everything. Implementing this idea, however, would turn formal, state-run education on its head!

Bethany has been spending seven hours a week travelling to and from secondary school. That's almost a whole working day. As a home educated student, she can now spend those hours in productive, creative pursuits of her choice, whether it be playing violin; belly dancing; learning German and French; studying artists; preparing wholefood meals; attending her graphic art for teens sessions at the library; pulling the amplifier out for a singing session; writing stories; chatting with, and learning from, women of all ages at the local knitting café; composing music at the piano; or watching Eliza having horse riding lessons with a teenage friend in the village.

When I pulled out my copy of School is Not Compulsory, to remind myself of the legal requirements when withdrawing a child from school, my daughters told me that home education means I mustn't forget that "cuddles are compulsory!" Fancy the little rascals thinking I'd forgotten that! So, I've got eight months of cuddles to catch up on ~ that should get me through an English Winter!

****

October, 2009: It's now two years since the girls have returned home from their brief time in school. They still talk about those days, but they're both clear that they'd never go back to an ordinary school. If we were wealthy or they had the chance of scholarships, they'd both be keen to explore life in a democratic, child-led school, (such as those based on the Sudbury model), for a year or so before university, if they choose to go. Despite, or because of, their freedom in learning, they both feel that tertiary education isn't likely to be necessary for their life paths. However, statistically, home educated students do very well in being accepted into tertiary educational institutions, and in how they perform during those years.

Our culture appears to be UNAWARE *of the impact of imposing education upon children.*

Local Education Authority

When the girls chose to go to school, I knew that that was the end of our complete freedom in unschooling, as up until that point the Local Education Authority didn't have a record of us. As soon as they left school, I had a letter from the LEA wanting to know: how we home educate, what subjects we covered, lesson plans and everything else which is counter to unschooling!

The two annual reports we've submitted have been very well received. Every country has its own rules and regulations about home education, some going as far as to make it illegal (Germany).

School days: admiring their school lunches. An abundance of fruit, salad vegetables and stuffed vine leaves.

In the UK, though, it would appear the vast majority of LEAs don't have a grasp of unschooling/totally autonomous learning, so the way around this is to tell them what they want to hear in a way *they understand*: that your children are doing core subjects, *and* socialising. Tell them this, and tell them a thousand other things of interest. Avoid filling in *their* forms and answering *their* questions about timetables, subjects, etc.; and present your own documents, complete with illustrations, recipes, musical compositions, diary dates of adventures and social outings, and anything else that shows your children aren't locked in a cupboard all day.

The LEA inspectors have a responsibility to ensure home educated children aren't being neglected, emotionally or educationally.

As a parent, you have a responsibility to raise your children consciously.

Nurturing the Nature!

I've long wondered about nature vs. nurture, and which one is our foundation as human beings. I've come to the conclusion that we arrive with a very definite nature (based on genetics, soul choices, womb life, and so on), and that the way we're nurtured can greatly hinder or help us to become the best version of ourselves.

My passion for psychological astrology has allowed me to study the psyche not only of myself and my family, but also of friends and strangers. In doing so, I've discovered that our wiring and perceptions are fairly firmly in place, but that each and everyone of us has the ability to transcend the limitations in our way, as well as to transform ourselves despite handicaps which show up in life.

Whether we like it or not, the education system is a form of 'nurture'. It acts as a surrogate parent, a *symbiotic* relationship, informing our children with ideas, beliefs and patterns about life. School shapes us. School praises us (if we're lucky!), and school knocks us flat. School repeatedly tells us where we're 'not good enough'. Not good enough for whom or what?

School dictates our early life, and can impact on the *rest of our lives*, whether we're conscious of it or not.

As an unschooling parent, I realise the power and responsibility in my role not only as a parent, but as someone who is influencing the stage and platform upon which my young girls are building the foundation of their lives. As a family, we're like a minority control group, showing the world how children can grow without school and formal education, and thrive in the world. Our culture doesn't want to hear this message, but before long it won't have much choice. The tipping effect will throw the balance towards an autonomous childhood.

Family is community, and although it's a small community, it's the most important one we'll ever live in. It's here that we find mirrors for our behaviour; where we develop beliefs and prejudices; where our passions are nurtured or negated; where our principles shape us. At some point, we may want to smash the mirror, or buff it up to shine more. Ideally, it's a safe place for our growth. Not everyone has that luxury, but I do hope my children become adults who value the start they were given in life: growing in a space of love.

One of the most inspiring women I know is Siobhán, a friend in Ireland. She's the oldest of ten home educated children, and is now home educating her own children. When the world tells me what I'm doing is crazy, I just remember her beautiful face, giving heart, and ageless wisdom. And I remind myself that she didn't go to school. When we aren't caught up in culture's messages, we're are able to live authentic lives.

As a family, we're like a minority control group, showing the world how children can grow without school and formal education, and thrive in the world.

Our culture doesn't want to hear this message, but before long it won't have much choice.

The tipping effect will throw the balance towards an autonomous childhood.

Home Business

"Home Sweet Homebirth". I remember, when pregnant, being behind a car in a carpark and spying a bumper sticker which read: Home Sweet Homebirth. I loved it, and jumped out to ask the owner where she got her groovy sticker from. Those three simple words spoke so much to my heart. Home is sweet, and even sweeter when our babes are born there.

Over the years, our lifestyle has evolved from Paul working out of the home ~ and being absent from the family for five to seven days a week in order to make ends meet, at times ~ to being home-based, with me and our children. It's not uncommon for unschoolers to start questioning the insanity of our cultural expectation that fathers remain away from their families all day. There have been financial compromises to get to this place, but it's completely worth it. This feels like *family living* now.

Our home this past decade, while being located in a glorious location, hasn't been the home of our dreams, but the home of our 'means'. Regardless, it's been a haven to nurture our dreams. And for this, I'm thankful.

In many ways, home education is an extension for us of the ideals of home birth. Home is where the heart is, a sacred place to gather and nurture loved ones; a place to feel safe and loved, and to give love. Birthing babies in the home where they were conceived, with love, is a beautiful experience that permeates the journey of parenting for many, many years. And likewise, having a home business continues this theme. For us, this recognition of 'right livelihood' and recognising our talents, and the gifts we offer this world, provides a living example to our children.

By working at home, there's no separation of our life's work from the rest of our life. Home has a vibrational energy that I'd be hard pressed to find in an office. Sure, I could take family photos in for my desk, but what about the music of my choice; the aroma of home-made soup on the stove; the cuddles from my children throughout the day, and not just at either end of it; the cups of tea made by my husband; the red squirrel and red-breasted robin in the poplar tree outside my window? Home-based work means that when the Sun shines, I don't have to look longingly out the window, and feel like a victim. I scoop my work up, and sit in the sunshine! And some days I don't work at all. Working from home means that our children have both parents available, even if one of them is busy. There's always someone there to take them to the swimming pool, library, market, for a walk, listen to music practice or to kick a ball.

When families work from home, they're more invested in their local community than when they're absent eight hours a day. Sometimes I walk past homes in our village where both parents work full-time, and I think it's such a shame there's no one inside to enjoy their beautiful home and garden.

If the idea of a home-based business appeals to you, but seems financially daunting, then consider this: working away means commuting costs, lunches out, someone to care for your children when you're at work, wardrobe, and so on. Self-employment makes great financial sense when you invest in the services of a savvy accountant. As our accountant says to us, "I'm the gamekeeper, not the poacher!"

If I were to make a suggestion about working from home, it would be this: *do what you're passionate about.* Many home businesses begin from hobbies. You're an example to your children, so don't let them see you slaving away at something in which your soul's not firmly invested.

I've been awed by the ingeniousness of many subscribers to The Mother magazine: women who've been at home all day, but also wanted to contribute to their family's income while being 'mum'. I've seen businesses grow from cotton nappies, cloth menstrual pads, mother-child artwork, doula-ing, hand-made cards, mentoring, writing books and self-publishing, bed & breakfast, music teaching, garden design, clothes making and redesign, and so much more. It's not limited to arts and crafts, though. Families learn to think outside the box, and question how they can bring their skills as lawyers, debt advisors, yoga teachers, celebrants, veterinary surgeons, publicists, midwives, osteopaths, to the world ~ while working from home and being available for their family.

Childhood is Not an Apprenticeship

*"The girls do a lot of work around the farm.
That's part of learning, too."*
Mrs Ingalls to Mrs Olsen, Little House on the Prairie.

Childhood's not an apprenticeship for adult life. Our early years are real, and no less valid than when we're in our twenties or fifties.

Every moment is an opportunity to learn ~ for parent and child. Unschooling is never just about the children. It's a complete way of life for everyone within the family. I can't imagine any personal growth course being as rich as the journey I've been on for the past fourteen years.

We have great days, and we have not so great days, but we remember this is about family dynamics, and not about education. Bad days should never be used as leverage to think institutional learning might be better for our kids.

Our goal, I believe, is to let go of the need to always identify the learning opportunities. We need to just let them happen; to trust the process.

Bethany at three years old.

Aged 3 and 5, riding their little bikes through the village. Summer, 2000.

Simple Abundance

Summer, 2004 ~ The Mother magazine, Issue 10

One of the things I really love about not sending my kids to school is the fact that it reduces their chances of not appreciating all the good things in their life! Peer pressure, just as television advertising, can cause untold stress in families because a child feels the 'need' to own a certain brand item. This struck me the other day when the girls were waiting for Paul to fix their bikes. They were given by an older girl in the village who'd outgrown hers, and by another friend. They're very rusty bikes. They're old bikes; squeaky bikes; not glamorous bikes. These bikes get us from A to B, and the chain usually comes off somewhere in-between, with one or all of us having to push our bikes home! My girls LOVE their bikes. They've never once said they couldn't possibly be seen on such outdated rust-buckets.

They've never once been ungrateful for having a bike that doesn't have the best brand name on it. Nor have they fussed about them not gleaming with shiny paint.

I've watched the girls develop their confidence on these bikes as they hurtle round the village. We've known for some time that they needed new bikes ~ for no other reason than that they're growing up so quickly, and have outgrown them. Preferring to re-use or recycle items, I knew it was just a matter of time before some 'new' bikes would come our way. And sure enough, last week, I saw a sign in the local Co-op ~ Two bikes for 7-10 year olds, £10 each.

What luck! They were still available. And bike helmets thrown in, too. Wouldn't you know it, though, the rain pelted down the morning Bethany and Eliza were set to ride their new bikes. That didn't stop them disappearing outside in their pyjamas.

I peeked out from the upstairs bathroom window, to see them both sitting in the boot of the car stroking the pedals of their new bikes. Bless them! Bikes which, I might add, are at least 10 years old. To my girls, these are new bikes. They're much bigger. And they are boys' bikes. My girls don't care! For me, their healthy attitude is worth celebrating.

Their carefree unschooling days bring many opportunities for natural learning. There's something about extending one's physical skills that builds on itself, leading from strength to confidence, and a belief one can achieve anything. The girls spent about a month climbing on top of the hen house roof ~ then they would 'dare' each other to "walk the ridgepole". They came across this idea in the story of Anne of Green Gables, and love to enact it! One day, they seemed to realise that they could use the hen house roof as a stepping stone to get on top of what will be the donkey barn. That's the point when a mother's heart sinks. I have to bite my tongue quite often, and remind myself that I was a thousand times more daring and adventurous when I was their age. I probably was only able to do half of what I did because my mother was unaware of what I was up to!! I had more acreage to explore, and was able to easily vanish from her sight! I'm sure her motherly instincts would have prevented me doing a lot of things. Adventure and risk- taking build character in a child. It leads to a sense of achievement that has a far more profound effect than scoring 10 out of 10 in a test. Why? Because when we set our own agenda, it has value and meaning, and we're doing it for the most important person in our world: ourselves. Performing well in a test (as a child) is rarely for us, but nearly always for a teacher or parent.

It's the extending of ourselves and testing our limits, which make us feel good. Feeling good raises our serotonin levels, and acts as an anti-depressant. Inevitably this builds healthy self-esteem. I believe that the huge increase in childhood depression could have been eliminated if such children had a life outside television and computers, and four walls.

Paul and I are acutely aware of how quickly our little girls are growing. We treasure the family bike rides, and the fact we sit down to eat meals as a family. It won't always be like this. In the next decade, my daughters will grow from young girls to adults, and could well have left home if they've inherited any of my sense of adventure. I've got just ten years to provide them with an environment in which they can explore their place in the world while still having the safety net of home.

I've no regrets about not imposing their brief childhood into an institutional setting. The hardest part has always been fielding the well intended or grossly misguided comments from others who have no concept of the benefits of a school-free life.

A Mountainous Milestone

Autumn, 2004 ~ The Mother magazine, Issue Eleven

It's amazing how when your babes are tiny, each milestone is huge. Every new development is documented, if not on paper, at least in memory: the excitement of the first crawl, or sitting up; the first pearly white appearing after endless nights of no sleep. Milestones are many when our children are babies. Even in the first couple of years, there's so much to watch out for. It's funny, though, how after a while we stop recording such things. Most baby journals tend to stop by age five.

We just get on with life then, don't we? It would be easy to believe the next major milestone in life is the onset of puberty. Not so! We've had two major milestones recently. The first was the all exciting family bike rides.

Our recent milestone was mountainous, to say the least: about eight kilometres climbing up and walking along the mountain. We live on the doorstep of the spectacular Lake District, but like many tourists, we've tended to just drive through and admire the tall mountains. They're rather beautiful. When a couple of local home educating families chose to do their monthly Sunday walk, I was quick to think we needed a day off work, and should have a family outing.

How I connected relaxation with a long walk up and down a mountainside is beyond me ~ but there you go, spontaneity has been my downfall in life more than once!

My kids loved it. The first mile or two straight up hill was particularly rugged. It was along a bridle path: no horse could have made it up that rocky creek! Bethany and Eliza ran. They were excited. Full of joy...and "Mum, this is so wonderful!" They've been wanting to mountain climb for a while, and I promised that soon enough it would happen.

At some point there'd be a tarn they could swim in and picnic beside. Nothing like a dangling carrot for when excited legs become limp with over-use! We tramped through peat bogs, up rock edges, climbed a ridge, mum and dad puffed and panted: but still the girls trooped on. They scampered up a rocky ledge, I scraped the skin off my leg, and got pushed up by two burly men. Not good! Not a milestone for me! But this mountain walking milestone marks another important point in our journey as a family. It allows us to do more adventurous activities than, say, a year ago. I've mentioned before the importance of stretching our physical selves in order to increase one's self esteem. Climbing such a mountain enabled the girls to experience their own endurance skills, and then be rewarded by a magnificent view: a view which could only ever be *imagined* from down below. They discovered cliff edges, and what height really means (while mother stepped backwards to thwart vertigo!). Finding new and unusual wild flowers growing in unlikely places, and pockets of dark, deep water, added to their journey.

They learnt how to estimate the water's depth by the ripples caused from a thrown pebble. I appreciate how much my children value wildlife, and their natural inquisitiveness regarding the world around them. Put my children in Nature's playground, and you'll see their true selves emerge: curious, playful, delighted, enthralled. Give them dirt, flowers, rocks, sand, algae, water ~ and you have the ingredients for a childhood of fun. Nature is the one constant companion as they've moved along their journey of milestones. Now they've added mountains to their play-kit, all sorts of adventures await!

Jake the Peg

Spring, 2005 ~ The Mother magazine, Issue Thirteen

My daughters have just discovered the Australian entertainer, Rolf Harris. And I'm just about to discover how many times a mother can hear *Jake the Peg* before officially being certified insane. Today will almost certainly be the day. Eliza insists on putting this particular song on repeat. The idea of a dad having difficulty changing the nappy of a baby with three legs is, to my girls, riotous.

Eventually I realise that if I can't beat 'em, I've simply got to join 'em. So I do my best *Jake the Peg* impersonation, jumping around the room ~ which leads to them dissolving into complete hysterical laughter. But wait! There's a HUGE problem. This couldn't possibly be the same room that I tidied from top to bottom just this morning. Could it? There's no room to jump around easily as *Jake the Peg*. I'm surrounded by paper, cotton reels, wooden toys, coat hangers (coat hangers?), pencils, a plate of almonds, orange peels, sticks, wool, three pairs of scissors, magazine proof reading (ok, that's my fault, not theirs), crocheted dolls. This room is a mess. This room is what unschooling seems to represent in our house.

Finally Eliza turns off the CD, and sits down to play cards with Bethany and Alfie.

They've decided to play the 21 game. It's something Paul taught them to help with the process of learning to count in their head. Some would say that was a creative way of doing it. Me, I think it's downright sneaky!

Alfie is Paul's ventriloquist doll. He doesn't look a day older than when Paul found him in a market about 29 years ago, when his eldest daughter, Hannah, was just a babe. Paul has been using him professionally for just about as many years, entertaining kids in shopping malls. He's proved to be an interesting addition to the family ~ Alfie, that is, not Paul. He spends a good deal of his time stuffed into a suitcase. When Bethany was little, she was dead scared of him. Eliza, however, even from a few months of age, adored him, and always wanted to touch him. The day Eliza really discovered her true power was when she pulled his head off, and Bethany ran screaming from the room.

Now the girls are older, and both of them absolutely adore Alfie, Paul is showing them his insides. Eliza has taken to mastering the physical aspect of Alfie. Next they'll be learning to ventriloquise. She's spending a good deal of time talking to me with her lips not moving.

Learning the unusual art of ventriloquism has highlighted one of the joys of home educating. It means the girls can spend hours and hours on discovering, exploring, questioning, investigating, learning and digesting new information, and developing skills. There's no restriction by the use of timetables.

The mild Spring weather has seen us back outside again. Hoorah! We're working over the spiral herb garden. The girls love to help with their copper garden tools. Eliza counted more than 30 worms yesterday in an area about a foot wide. She adores animals and creatures of any description. Sitting right in the middle of freshly prepared soil, Eliza declared herself a Worm Tamer. She was even telling Bethany and I what worms smelt like! It's these moments, working and playing together in the sunshine, that really sum up the more enjoyable side of home education: the feeling of freedom as we structure our own day in terms of when we work, when we play, when we eat, when we rest.

Out here in the gorgeous Spring sunshine, birds whistling and grass growing, I forget that I can't cross the lounge room floor!

Eliza, the Worm Tamer.

Missouri Riddle or Singing Chef?

When Eliza grows up, there's no shortage of life paths for her to follow. She's imagined owning a vegan café in Italy, and having an alpaca farm. The thought of being Prime Minister of England so she can change the country appeals to her, but she's more drawn to travelling the world with her saxophone and doing concerts, or being a film actress. Her proposed saxophone stage name is Rainbow Robinson. In the meantime, she's building her repertoire so she can go busking. Eliza's imagining carrying her sax on the back of her bike, with a willow bike basket on the front to collect her busking money.

Last year, she was Psychic Eliza, and read tarot cards for guests at a May Day celebration near Oxford (at my sister's pub). Eliza was right at home, with her head covered in a scarf, big hoop earrings, and a velvet cloth on the table as she lay her divination cards down to predict people's fortunes.

For now, she's Queen of the Kitchen, and her animals of choice are two cats. She's working on her parents to bring a third cat into the family.

For three years or so now, Eliza's been developing her passion for preparing botanical cuisine. She not only loves to make a meal, but is enthusiastic about growing food, and understanding the nutritional elements of what she's eating, as well as discovering more about the benefits of herbs.

The geographical and cultural origin of food is of great interest and fascination to her, and she's spent much time studying this.

For the past ten years, we've lived in a cottage so tiny you'd think it was designed for the characters in The Borrowers. The kitchen is the smallest room. This has proved to be a blessing and a curse. The cursing times were when Eliza was there beside me *all the time* wanting to see how I was preparing foods, then psychically booting me out of the kitchen. "I KNOW how to do it! Leave me alone!" she'd say, stamping her nine year old feet. In the end, the personality clash (two 'leaders' in the postage stamp-sized kitchen) was not a path to peace and happiness; and so I learned to remove myself, and trust her to be able to do whatever she needed to do in there without burning herself or setting the house on fire.

Eliza's food passion extended into sharing her recipes in The Mother magazine, with a regular column; and now she's exploring food photography.

If she's not cooking for a career, or managing an animal rescue centre, then expect to see her historical novel, Missouri Riddle, in a bookshop near you.

Eliza and Bethany baking vegan choc chip muffins.

The Hit Musical, Fashion Designer, Rock Chick or Psychologist?

Like Eliza, Bethany's had the option to explore her various interests, and to discover new ones. Primarily, they have been in the arts: namely music and writing. She's attended a graphic arts course for teenagers; youth theatre; stage play-writing; choir; and has lessons for piano and violin. Bethany has found a niche, at the moment, in composing music, lyric writing and writing stage plays. Every day she finds herself absorbed in some aspect of this creation. There's no reason, if she followed this path, that she couldn't be a female version of Andrew Lloyd Webber. Bethany also loves the idea of writing musical scores for movies.

She's teaching herself rock guitar and flute, and is talking about acquiring a drum kit. Bethany's learning style is visual: pictures; textures; feeling. It's no surprise that she's so strongly drawn to the combination of writing, music and acting, and then drawing it all together into the 'picture' of musical theatre.

Bethany's become fascinated with psychology, psychological astrology, numerology, and the Enneagram of Personality Types. She's studying graphology (the interpretation of personality through handwriting). The direction she chooses to go is entirely hers. As parents, our investment is in her happiness and well-being. Clearly, if we see latent talents, we feel it's our job to help her look into those; but the key is to shine a light on them, not force her into a tunnel.

Eliza and Bethany, the Poncho Girls, late Autumn on the village green, Glassonby, Cumbria.

My Girls

This is what I hope my girls remember about their life without school: that they read for hours by the fireside, with hot carob or chocolate, or under plum trees with home-made lemonade from fresh limes, lemons and agave syrup, or up a field with a picnic, in bed by lamplight (sometimes moonlight, when I'd ordered lights out).

I pray they remember walking amongst wildflowers in the Summer, and picnics by Talkin Tarn. May the memories of all the dolls cut into life on the lounge room floor live in their hearts as part of their playful childhood.

Will they remember the seeds they've planted into the vegetable beds, and the joy they experienced every time they picked a bean, tomato, cucumber, sweetcorn or courgette? I hope so.

May the stains of fruits so abundantly juicy ~ blueberries, strawberries, raspberries and gooseberries ~ be a pleasant colouring to their souls.

When they're nursing and nourishing their own children ~ whether they're flesh and blood grandchildren for Paul and I, or grand life projects ~ please let them feel, within every cell of their being, that both their parents were there for them.

At night, when they close their eyes beneath starry skies, whether near or far, let the cuddles and long chats and riotous laughter that we shared on the family bed for so many years, bring warmth, wonder and wistfulness to their hearts. May they be comforted throughout their life's journey by the gifts they were given in the years without school. Unschooling, at its core, is about relaxed parenting. We trust the process of life to bring us our Highest good, and that we're part of the lovely rhythm and flow of life.

This book circles the seasons. I began in Winter, and we danced through our lives in Spring, Summer, Autumn, and as we prepare for publication, Winter is with us again. The journey of unschooling is no different: there are times for inward reflection, cosied up by the fire; moments of dynamic new life and brilliance, like the fresh leaves and new seedlings of Spring; the eager anticipation, followed up by the culmination of that energy and life force, in a warm and abundant Summer; and then, the harvest of our labours.

PART TWO
by Veronika Sophia Robinson

Bethany playing about in the rhubarb patch.
Sure beats Nursery School!

Spring

April showers. Shall we hang the washing outside, or not? Will the fruit trees survive the hail storms? We've enjoyed weeks, now, of ever increasing warmth, but today it's snowing? Will our saladlings survive? How many more frosts can our young vegetables endure? Do we have enough firewood left over from Winter?

Ostara and Easter

We've enjoyed carrying on a tradition from my childhood where my mother wrapped up parcels of healthy

Eliza and Bethany in their Easter bonnets, among the daffodils.

snacks and treats in coloured cellophane. Each parcel had the name of a different child. Our sub-tropical garden was huge, and more often than not, we found someone else's Easter treasure parcel before our own ~ and had to keep quiet!

I've never taught my daughters the Christian meaning of Easter (whether that be of a man on the cross with nails, or rotting one's teeth with Cadbury's chocolates brought by fluffy bunnies) ~ culture's managed to pass on that message loudly enough ~ but rather, I've shared with them the metaphysical interpretation of the crucifixion and resurrection.

We crucify ourselves each time we 'put ourselves down', and we resurrect ourselves when we affirm our goodness. Couldn't this well be the foundation of unschooling? Believe in yourself, and what you do, and you'll rise high… Grade yourself, put yourself down, and you crucify your essential self.

Ostara is the Goddess of Springtime and fertility. Christians derived the word Easter from Ostara, and the meaning of it comes from the Sun rising on the Eastern horizon.

Ostara is called upon when we wish to embark on new projects, and Spring is such a wonderful time for doing so. Spring reminds us that there's now light shining on us, and as a result we feel more vibrant. We may wear brighter coloured clothes, or have colourful flowers in the home. Ostara is the resurrection from the long, dark winter.

Spring Equinox

We're so blessed to live within easy walking distance of an ancient Druids' stone circle. Equinoxes and Solstices are times in our family to walk to the circle.

Spring is a time for enjoying much longer walks than those we've taken in Winter. It's a season to sip tisanes in the garden while soaking up the sunshine.

Each season, we create a Nature Table, or altar. In Spring, we decorate with Spring flowers, shoots and young leaves. A candle represents the new light.

Mushroom Soup

The best mushroom soups I've ever had are those which live in my childhood memories. After the Spring rains, mushrooms would grow wild all over the fields on my childhood property. My siblings and I would bring home buckets full, and our mother would make the most mouth-watering soups from them. I don't know her recipe, but this is similar, and was thoroughly enjoyed at one of our Mother magazine camps.

(serves a family of four)
200g wild mushrooms (available dried, in good health stores)
500g sliced mushrooms
2 cups onions, finely chopped
4 cups of liquid from vegetable bouillon
Freshly ground black pepper
Olive oil
3 tablespoons of curly leaf parsley for stirring in just before serving

Soak the dried wild mushrooms for an hour or so before adding to the soup. Include the soak water. Sauté the onions until clear, and set aside while frying the mushrooms. Add the vegetable bouillon. You may need more than four cups of liquid, depending on how long you've been cooking the soup for. Season with pepper, and add finely chopped parsley to the soup before serving.

Spring
By Eliza

If you go down to the woods today,
You'll be in for a big surprise…
The trees are green, the meadow's in bloom
The birds are back
There's rain on the woodland track.
The lambs are drinking from their mothers' breast
The birds are singing in their nest.

Grandmother's Potato Salad

My mother has such a lot to answer for ~ filling my memories with delicious foods from childhood. Those that I've been able to recreate to some degree have been passed on to my daughters, such as this potato salad.

waxy salad (early) potatoes (2 or 3 per person)
2 onions, finely chopped or grated
1 cucumber (mother uses tinned cucumber, but we use fresh, and mari-
nate it in apple cider vinegar for an hour before adding to the salad)
vegan mayonnaise
salt and pepper according to taste

Boil the potatoes with their skins on. Once tender and cooled, remove skins, and roughly chop potatoes into mouth sized pieces. Set aside.

Combine onions, finely diced cucumber, salt, pepper and enough mayonnaise to mix through potatoes. When well mixed, carefully add the potatoes. Allow to cool in the fridge before serving. It's very more-ish.

Springtime on the village green.

Spring Birthday

One of our birthday traditions has been using a birthday ring, made from wood, with holes in for candles and wooden animals, as a feature on the birthday table.

Although it was Autumn when I gave birth to Bethany, in Auckland, New Zealand, on March 13th, 1996, she's celebrated most of her birthdays in Spring. One of her favourite cakes was Italian apple and almond cake, but usually she asks for this delicious carrot cake.

Pineapple, Date and Carrot cake with cinnamon frosting

2 cups plain flour
1 teaspoon cinnamon
¼ teaspoon nutmeg
¼ teaspoon sea salt (Maldon)
1 teaspoon bicarbonate soda
2 teaspoons baking powder
2/3 cup dates, finely chopped
1 cup walnuts, roughly chopped
4 T egg replacer (mixed with a little water)
1 cup agave syrup
1 cup light olive oil
2 cups carrots, grated
2 cups of tinned pineapple, chopped

Mix together the oil, agave and egg replacer, then add the nuts, pineapple, dates and carrots. Add the flour, raising agents, salt, nutmeg and cinnamon. Pour into cake tin/s, and bake at 180 C for half an hour to 45 minutes, depending on oven type.

Cinnamon frosting

One tub Tofutti plain cream cheese, melted slightly in a bain marie, with two tablespoons of agave syrup, and ½ teaspoon of cinnamon mixed in well. When the cake has cooled, spread mixture around sides and across top. Decorate with a daffodil or other spring blossoms!

Dandelion Queens

My mother was the first person to teach Bethany and Eliza about eating dandelion leaves. In fact, when they think of her it's one of their first memories.

Dandelions are beautiful: first with their bright yellow flowers, and then with their fluffy ball-like seed tops, which beg anyone, young or old, to blow them off with a wish. The girls and I have made many a wish upon the breath blown against dandelion seeds. The flowers come out from about April, and can continue right up until December, depending on the severity of the weather. Most commonly found along roadsides, they're always in fields and meadows. Medicinally, they're brilliant for treating gall-bladder and liver complaints. The leaves are diuretic: ideal for treating skin issues, such as acne and eczema.

We use the leaves in vegetable juices, salads, and sometimes cooked, like spinach, with other vegetables.

Dandelion is excellent for purifying the blood. To do so, place about two teaspoonfuls in a cup of boiling water. Simmer for a minute or two. You can drink two cups a day for a month or so.

One of the girls' favourite songs when they were young was *Dandelion, Yellow As Gold*. It was sung each day on our walks.

Mum sings:
O dandelion, yellow as gold, what do you do all day?

Bethany & Eliza:
I just wait here in the tall green grass, till the children come to play.

Mum:
O dandelion, yellow as gold, what do you do all night?

Bethany & Eliza:
I wait and wait till the cool dews fall, and my hair grows long and white.

Mum:
And what do you do when your hair is white, and the children come to play?

Bethany and Eliza:
They take me up in their dimpled hands, and blow my hair away.

We discovered this catchy tune in a wonderful book called *Sing through the Day*. The song was written by Noreen Bath, and was the soundtrack to my daughters' early years.

Dandelion notation, hand-written by Bethany.
Sketch of children collecting dandelions, by Eliza.

Eliza, self-medicating with flower essences and homeopathy.

The Herb Garden

The jumbled herb garden under the eucalyptus tree isn't huge, but it does have what we need for culinary and medicinal purposes. The girls have grown up with a keen understanding of what herbs taste and smell like, both fresh and dried, and what they can be used for.

As a family, we don't run to the doctor for treating ailments. We nurture good health through conscious eating, walking outside in Nature regularly, and having happy relationships.

We look at illness as a message from our deeper self about what we're neglecting in terms of self-care and attention, and see our body's messages as wise.

On our journey, we've incorporated vibrational medicines such as colour healing, homeopathy, flower essences, herbs, teas and tinctures, mind/body nutrition, as well as the Hawaiian healing model, Ho'oponopono. We also have fortnightly chiropractic adjustments. This is an example of the diversity of unschooling, and how we learn from life. By taking care of the well-being of our body and mind, we find we honour other aspects of our life.

My mother used colour healing with me and my siblings. For example, dark blue was used to help ease my school headaches, and red was used to bring confidence to my shy brother. Yellow helped me to stop wetting my bed when I was about ten years old. A colour can be used in various ways, such as putting coloured cellophane around a light bulb, or using coloured solar water. My mother would use glass jugs of various colours, and put our bore water in them and leave the water out in the sunshine for a few hours. The light of the Sun would go through the coloured glass and infuse the water with the energy of the colour in question. While most children are given Calpol or some equivalent drug for headaches or fevers, I was given blue solarised water. We have used blue water with Bethany and Eliza.

Homeopathy is helpful for no end of diseases, ailments and anxieties. Bethany has used *Arg-nit* for pre-music exam nerves, with great success. When Eliza was about eight years old, she and Bethany were allowed to walk around certain parts of town without me. Usually they went from the bookshop to the library or health store. I was having some lovely leisure time in the bookshop when I heard an almighty scream in the lane below. No one had to tell me that it was Eliza. She always ensures she's heard, regardless of the situation. But what on Earth would be causing that shriek? A dog bite! Our resident dog lover had petted the wrong canine at the wrong time, and her skin was punctured. Most people would immediately think "Is the tetanus shot up to date?" or "Thank goodness she's had her tetanus jab." As we're a non-vaccinating family, such a thought wouldn't enter my head. Instead, because we work *with* the body, rather than against it, we gave Eliza the homeopathic remedy for bites: *Ledum*. Homeopathy has often been used in our family for bites, stings, dentistry, splinters and wounds. We've used *Ant. Tart* and *Drosera* for ongoing coughs, *Sepia* for PMT, and *Arnica* for bruises, dental work and severe back pain. *Lachesis* has proved effective for treating a dental abscess, and *Coffea* for dealing with severe nerve pain and headaches.

Instead of anti-biotics, such as for a tooth abscess, we use propolis (tree resin). It's one of Nature's strongest biotics, and is also a great anaesthetic ~ without side effects!

Magical Potions

For years, my daughters have played around making potions. As they've grown older, they've discovered that there's no limit to the potions and lotions which can be made at home and used instead of commercial products: soap, shampoo, face masks, cleansers, toners, lip gloss, deodorants, conditioners, facial scrubs...

Spring Onion and Quinoa Tabbouleh

Tabbouleh is traditionally made with cracked wheat, but since we keep wheat to a minimum in our diet, we use quinoa for this recipe instead. Quinoa (pronounced keen-wa) is a South American grain (a seed, really) high in protein, so it's a welcome addition to a vegetarian diet that's commonly debunked as 'not safe nutritionally' for growing children. It's very versatile, and can be used in place of rice, wheat, and even oats, for porridge. It cooks very quickly.

1 cup cooked quinoa
4 tablespoons fresh lemon juice
½ teaspoon fresh mint
5 spring onions
½ cucumber, finely diced
1 cup cherry tomatoes, cut in half
¼ cup finely chopped parsley
½ cup Greek black olives, chopped in half
5 tablespoons olive oil
1 ½ cloves of crushed garlic

Simply add all the ingredients to the cooked (drained) quinoa. Allow it to sit for half an hour or so before serving, so the flavours can mingle.

Rosemary Shampoo

We've a gorgeous rosemary bush in our garden, that's blessed us medicinally, in the kitchen, and in the bathroom.

50 grams of rosemary leaves (or a few drops of essential oil of rosemary if you haven't got a bush in your garden)
50 grams dried Irish Moss

Mix the leaves and dried moss together. Add 600 ml of boiled water, and allow it to cool. Strain, and use the liquid as a shampoo. It will feel slimy, but it'll leave your hair just lovely! If you prefer to have a soapy shampoo, add 100 grams of dried soapwort before pouring on the water.

Eliza and Bethany at the bottom of the garden.
Bethany and Eliza drawing on a Winter's day.

A Day in our Life

Summer, 2003 ~ The Mother magazine, Issue 6

May 15th, 2003
Lunar Eclipse in Scorpio
8.30am: I need the car today, so the girls and I drive Paul to work, which is about 12 miles from our home. "We don't want you to go to work" the girls chorus, as he waves goodbye.

We slip into town, and they help me get some postage done. We don't stay in town long because I'm going to Carlisle later in the morning. My mother will care for the girls while I'm at a radio interview. BBC Radio Cumbria has invited me to speak on the Midday Show about a new study just published which states that young children left in nurseries by their working mums suffer no emotional problems as a result. A flawed study in many ways, but that's worthy of another article. I'm away for three hours.

The girls are sitting in the front garden with my mum when I return. They're all busy making things.

3pm: The sun is shining. It's so deliciously warm following the ground frost this morning. Bethany and Eliza are busy, busy, busy in the back garden now. We've planted some lettuces, spinach and fennel. The Moon is in the sign of Scorpio ~ a water sign, good for planting 'leafy' plants.

Eliza is joyously watering our new garden of vegetables with her red watering can. She's in her element with soil and water. Various mud pies line the wooden borders of the vegetable garden.

Bethany's naked. Imagine a seven year old naked at school? I don't think so! "Why are you naked?" I ask her, curiously, without any hint of disapproval or casting of shame. I adore the sight of her beautiful body, and will not perpetuate the pathetic label of 'rudie' so often thrown with purposeful arrow by adults. She'll learn in a shameless way about societal hang ups. "Because it's fun!" she answers, as if it's the most obvious thing in the world. Her face lights up. "I want to feel the Sun on my skin." She must have inherited my Aussie blood.

Insects are hovering lazily, drugged by the warmth, as they dance the slow dance of Spring through unmown grasses and wildflowers. The birds in the pines and holly trees are sounding simply exquisite. How blessed we are ~ a free musical gift. I write these words at our picnic table, beneath the dappled shade of the plum tree ~ the Seductress of Summer already dangling tiny plums above us. My children are happy. Their senses are engaged. And that's when it hits me. THUD! My kids, *my kids*, had I made a different choice, could have missed this glorious day. They may not have experienced the beauty around them if I'd taken the expected path of sending them to school. Instead, they'd be sitting in unnatural positions: their small, growing bodies forced into hard chairs, beneath fluorescent lighting, and being taught the same information, at the same time, as thirty other children ~ regardless of whether they were ready for it, or indeed, if they already knew it. They may have been force-fed ~ like the geese used to make foie gras ~ information and facts shoved down them, when their minds and hearts yearned for something as simple as daydreaming.

Daydreaming is vital for 'filling in' the pieces of information we've received. How often do teachers yell out to their students "stop daydreaming!"?

I was horrified to hear of a local nursery school which promotes computer use by tiny children. I'm in a minority, I know, but this is madness. One day parents will discover that this is the last thing that their child's growing mind and body needs. But sadly, by then it will be too late.

I don't want my children to be robots. I want them to be children. And to enjoy being children. I'm passionate about wanting them to feel, think, learn and express themselves as Nature designed them to do, not factory farmed under artificial lighting, with artificial food and artificial learning structures (aka the National Curriculum).

A caller to Radio Cumbria chose to wait until after I'd left the studio, to phone in and say how selfish she thought I was by keeping my children at home. Selfish? Since when is it selfish to dedicate your life to attending to your children's needs on a full-time basis? What's selfish about answering one hundred questions an hour, usually fired by both girls at the same time? I can't see any school teacher doing that. Is it selfish to allow your home to be a 'creative working environment' (read: messy) for the resident artists?

Ok, then, call me selfish. The well-being of my children is my priority. It comes before anything else in my life. Obviously the winner of 'mother of the century' is meant to be one who doesn't care about her kids, or want to raise them herself. Over the past year, I've come to discover a number of parents who've taken their children out of school as a direct result of reading my unschooling columns in The Mother. That's quite breathtaking. My words were/are never meant to be prescriptive, but to paint a picture of our family life. Really, I've no higher goal than to illustrate 'another' way. Each family which chooses to step out of The System (or indeed, never steps into it) will need to approach and experience unschooling in their own way.

I'm the first to admit that not every day is a picnic, but every day we can have a picnic! It might be up on our field, in the back garden, in the bath tub, snuggled on a rug by the fire, in a den of cardboard boxes in the bedroom, or in the car. It might be up by the stone circle or down at the woods; in the sunshine or under the Moon…

11pm: Tonight we celebrated the Lunar Eclipse, around a campfire on our land. We supped beneath a magical and majestic rising full Moon. We went there just after 7pm, the time when Paul is usually reading a bedtime story, or getting the girls tucked into bed. Tonight was different. And what the heck, a late night isn't going to affect their 'performance' at unschooling tomorrow.

Eliza helped me to transplant some sunflower seedlings as the Sun sank into a sea of apricot magic. She really enjoyed both experiences, and was conscious of the brilliant sunset without me having to point it out to her. Bethany, meanwhile, rolled down a hillside, well hidden in grasses and wildflowers three feet high. Best of all was when both girls giggled uncontrollably as they tried to balance themselves atop a huge straw bale that will eventually be used for mulching around the fruit trees. Their laughter was music to my heart.

Beneath Mother Moon, and by the dance of firelight, Grandmother Angelikah played her harmonica into the rapidly cooling night air of late Spring. She played to me just as beautifully, almost three decades ago, as I lay in bed drifting to sleep.

It's said that a parent needs to gift their child with two things: roots and wings. Like the tender seedlings I planted earlier in the evening, I'm here to comfort, make secure, and tend to my daughters; to offer strength and support to their vulnerable selves until such time as they're firmly rooted within their being and their world. Their wings are sprouting. I've no fear that they won't go off and fly, but just as a mother bird would never push a young chick from its nest before it had a good chance of flying, nor will I. If that makes me selfish, then darn it, I'm selfish and proud of it!

Eliza and Bethany performing a play underneath the pine trees.

Part Three

My Life
by Eliza Serena Robinson

I'm Eliza, and I was born in Auckland, on January 28th, 1998. I've been unschooled most of my life, apart from a couple of terms about three years ago. These are my thoughts on life without school, and about the differences between school and unschooling.

Baby videos and personality

A couple of months ago, when we were sorting out a cupboard, we found all the videos of when Bethany and I were little. When we watched those videos, I noticed that my personality when I was eight months old had aspects of what I'm like now. There's a bit in one of the videos where I was trying to climb a chair, and Bethany tried to help me; but little Eliza was independent, and pushed Bethany's arm off her, and managed to climb the chair. I've been able to climb chairs ever since, and I'm still quite independent.

Here are a few things which happened as a baby, some earlier than normal:
MY FIRST WORDS: I uv oo (I love you) at 10 months old.
MY FIRST SENTENCE: May I have an orange please, Mummy? (at 11 months old.)
MY FIRST SMILE: a few days old.
MY FIRST SONG: at 11 months old I hummed a song called Lemon drops and gum drops.
MY FIRST LAUGH: two weeks old.
MY FIRST STEPS: (my moment of fame) February 6, 1999 Dubai airport (to an international audience, with all the air hostesses clapping)

Grandmother

Grandmother lives in Australia, and would sometimes come over for a couple of months; I liked it when she came over. She'd take Bethany and I for walks, and put licorice or oranges in the churchyard or in the grass near the swings, and say that angels put them there. She also made Berliners (German doughnuts). They were *lovely*!!!!!!!!!! Once when she was here, she turned the old goose shed down the garden into a play house for Bethany and I to make mud pies in. Now the roof's fallen in because Bethany and I climbed on it. We played many games down there, and quite a few of the children in the village have made mud pies in that part of our garden.

The Big Freeze, January 2010, Cumbria. Below: Eliza's first painting, aged thirteen months.

Eliza's first painting
aged 13months
at Mansion house

Earthsong

I remember the time I planted the poultry wheat all over the ground in the polytunnel at Earthsong, the small piece of land we owned. The polytunnel is a warm place where things grow *very* quickly. Mum wasn't too pleased to have wheat coming up everywhere amongst her tender saladlings.

We had a small chicken shed, which was great for climbing on because it helped us to get on the roof of the barn. It was a great lookout to see across the fields all around us.

The berry garden had 100 blueberry bushes, hundreds of raspberry canes and gooseberries. The raspberries were of the variety called Autumn Bliss, which was such a treat in Autumn when most of the fruit and vegetables had been eaten.

There were so many vegetables we grew there: hundreds and hundreds of potatoes, broad beans, pumpkins, French beans, parsnips, carrots, onions, tomatoes, lettuce, cucumber, peppers, and aubergines. We grew asparagus between the fruit trees in the orchard. There was a kiwi fruit vine in the polytunnel, though it was too busy climbing to grow fruit.

The first Winter that we had Earthsong, my Mum, Dad, Bethany and I did lots of planting! We had hundreds of fruit trees. There were apples of many varieties, pears and plums. It was a freezing cold day that I thought would never end. We got all the trees planted, and now they produce lots of fruit. Our cat Bella is buried under one of the trees. It grows the best apples!

One of the funniest things that ever happened at Earthsong was when grandmother tried to grow a pineapple. She must have thought she was still in Australia! Her other trees are growing really well though, like walnuts, apricot and apples

Our friend Andri gave us five hens. We didn't get them for the eggs, but so they could enjoy the land, and leave their poo to fertilise the field. If you know Andri, then you'll know that what followed shouldn't have been a surprise! We'd been away in Italy for a week, and when we came back, each of our hens flew up onto the stone wall, and, in turn, they each began to crow. CROW! OH NO! NOT FIVE HENS? Five cockerels! We couldn't believe our ears. We were in shock. Mum shook her head, and then laughed: "ANDRI!!!"

What were we going to do with five cockerels? Everyone knows cockerels don't get along. We hoped that maybe because they didn't have hens around that they might all get along. Not so. They definitely had a pecking order. We named them Martin (Crowe), Roy (Orbison), Charlie (after Prince Charles) [blame Dad for those names!], Handsome, and Cock (as in cockerel!).

Charlie didn't crow. He wasn't allowed to because of his place as lowest in the pecking order, after losing a fight with Roy. And then one day, Dad was putting some spread on our home-baked bread (we used to eat lunch up at the land most days), and Charlie came and pecked it off Dad's lap. I have no idea what was in Mum's bread, but Charlie found his crow!! The other cockerels couldn't believe it, either. I used to carry Cock all the time; he used to whistle when I stroked him.

Martin and Roy didn't like being carried. We had so much fun at the land. Bethany and I would spend all day doing different things. We had a swing on the crab apple tree, and a really *big* swing next to the pond. We'd help plant and harvest fruit and vegetables, make mud pies, water trees, pick flowers and herbs, spread straw around trees, run, ride our bikes, build dens, paddle in the pond, and daydream. Almost every day we went to the land. Sometimes we took books, or pens and paper as well. Even if it was raining, we could still go up because we could shelter in the polytunnel, and do things while mum was working. Mum always made us a lunch so we could spend the day up there. The land's about 1.8 miles from our home, so it was a bit of a walk there and back each day. Good exercise!

I don't know what it is about boy animals and our family, but we adopted four kid goats that were going to get killed if a home wasn't found. We don't eat animals, so stories like that always pull on our heart strings. Dad rapidly put up fences so we could contain the goats for a bit. We soon discovered goats don't believe in fences. Ever! They were all boys. We hoped they'd eat grass ~ but goats don't believe in grass, either! They prefer fruit trees, willow trees, clothes, and human hair; actually, anything that's higher than them! But we loved them!

We ended up taking our goats to a local animal park, where they get to be visited by many children every day, and the fences are very high. The goats ~ Rimino, Hank, Beau and Chive ~ adjusted to their new home quickly, and Dad took us to visit them each week. Rimino died not long after. And a few days ago we found out another one had died. I'd love to get more goats some day. They're such sociable creatures. I hope to do some volunteer work at the donkey sanctuary, too.

Courses/groups

Bread making
We live about two miles from the Watermill, in Little Salkeld, where they stone-grind biodynamic grains. When I was about four, I did a bread baking course with some other home educators. A few years later, I did a craft course there. It's one of the few places in Cumbria where we can get the sort of food we like to eat, but it's still not as good as we eat at home.

Parlé vouz Francais?
I've been in two different French groups. One was specifically for home educators, and was held in the tutor's home. The other was in a village hall for children all around the villages.

Adult Night Classes
Two years ago, I signed up to do a night class for adults on 'healthy' vegetarian cookery. I was ever so excited to try new foods; but it turned out to be very disappointing, and I didn't go back after the night I vomited ~ it was the first time I'd been sick in seven years! The recipes weren't healthy, and were full of sugar and all sorts of other things we don't normally eat. I substituted rice milk for cows' milk, and egg replacer for eggs.

It seemed silly for Mum to drive me to town each week to make things that weren't challenging (I was always finished an hour before everybody else, and even had my washing up done). Because Mum lets me have free rein in the kitchen, I've learnt far more at home than any night course could have taught me.

Youth Theatre
In the Lake District is Keswick's Theatre by the Lake. Bethany and I have been to the youth theatre, and really enjoyed the classes. I'm about to join a drama academy for 12 to 17 year olds.

Angelikah and Eliza having a picnic at Lacey's Caves.

Penrith teenage reading group

Once a month, at the library in Penrith, there's a teenage reading group. We really enjoy it! The people there are very nice. The last time we were there, Bethany laughed so much her face resembled a beetroot!!!!!!!!!!!!!!!!!!!!!!!!!!!!!!!!

Musical Chairs

I had piano lessons for about a year, but I felt like the teacher always compared me with Bethany (who's two years older), which didn't make me feel very good: so I stopped going. I still play piano now, but I don't have lessons. One of the reasons I like piano, is that I can sing along while I play.

I'm now learning the saxophone. My neighbour, nicknamed 'musical John', has five saxophones, and lent me one for a while to see if I'd like it. I *love* it! I now have my own sax, and after six months of teaching myself, I have a teacher. She's great, and has a wonderful, dynamic nature. I've realised how important it is for me to have a teacher who is bright and has lots of energy and personality.

I've been saving up money, and recently bought a ukulele, which I'm teaching myself to play. The other night, we went to a concert called *The Guitar Whisperer*, and the musician, Richard Durrant, played all sorts of guitars, including a ukulele. He was amazing! I feel really inspired now.

"Who says you're not allowed to smile in a passport photo?

Just try and stop me!"

Adventures with the family

These are the some of the adventures we've had, as a family, over the years.

Italy

When I was six, we went to Italy, for a week. (Do you know that it takes less time to get to Italy from Glassonby than it does to London from Glassonby?) Our friend, Derek, sent us there to observe the 'café culture' so we could bring ideas back for his café. It's really hard work eating your way around Italy, you know!

The gay ice cream parlour twins gave us gelati samples because we were friends with friends of theirs. It was such a treat being offered flavour after flavour. Afterwards, we went and walked on the beach, even though it was Winter and freezing.

We travelled north, and stayed on an organic orchard. The highlight was being able to cuddle the newborn goats.

We learnt a bit of Italian before we went over, and impressed the staff at Ancona airport with our words.

It's really interesting that we made friends with Italian children when we couldn't understand each other's language. We managed to play really well, and it seemed we laughed a lot.

Ireland

We went to Ireland a few years ago because Mum was doing a talk about home education. The best part of going there for me was all the yummy food, and travelling through Wicklow National Park. It's really beautiful there.

Our friends live on a smallholding, off-grid. It's great to be in a place that doesn't use electricity or flushing toilets, because it makes you think about everything you take for granted, and about how differently we can do things. Alex makes amazing sourdough bread, and Siobhán is a lovely cook. They live in a bog with their two children. It was really interesting to walk in the bog, and see how different it is from other soil. We've just visited them again. I had a great time, especially sitting in their home-made hot tub for four hours! We also went to Dublin for my birthday lunch!

Manchester

For the past two Summers, Bethany's attended a Summer School for Strings in Manchester, run by the Royal Northern College of Music. Because we live about two hours drive from Manchester, and only have one car, we all end up going down for the whole week. My favourite things about Manchester are: the Manchester Wheel (it made Mum get vertigo! ~ Laughing!). I don't understand this, because she once rode a rollercoaster 36 times in a row! She says that she's scared of heights now because she's a Mum! I love the vegan food at the Buddhist café, delicious meals at Wagamama (it's a Japanese noodle bar), and the amazing health food store called On the Eighth Day. It's got the best vegan chocolate cake in the WHOLE world. The last time we went to Manchester, Dad did some busking.

Oxford

My aunty Heidi (that's mum's sister) lives near Oxford. She has a pub in a little village. We've been there a couple of times. Last time, she was having a village party for May Day, and asked Dad to come and sing. Bethany and I helped to run stalls, and I was Psychic Eliza, giving tarot card readings. People actually *paid me* for my fortune telling.

South Shields

We've been to South Shields quite a lot. Dad was born there, and Nana lived there until she died. I enjoyed going to the beach there, even in Winter. I'm sure we only ever go to the beach in the Winter!

Berwick upon Tweed

We don't have holidays very often, or get away, but one time we went to Berwick, and stayed at an organic B&B. We've got lots of photos of us on the beach ~ *in Winter!* On the way home, we stopped at Alnwick. The old railway station, which is absolutely huge, is now a second hand book store. We were in heaven; they even had biscuits there! There were more books than you could ever imagine. Mum was happy because she'd found a bunch of specialist astrology books that you'd never find in ordinary bookshops.

Back then, Bethany and I picked up lots of children's stories. It's a real treasure trove. I'd really like to go back there again and have a whole day exploring all the sections, especially now that I have specific interests.

Telford

Not long ago, Bethany and I went with Mum to Shropshire because she had a stall at a conference for Radical Midwives. Bethany
and I were excited because we got to stay in a hotel. When Mum
gives a talk somewhere on breastfeeding, we get to help sell books
and magazines, as well as meeting interesting people. This is great,
and we get to earn pocket money, too.

And, it means that there's a possibility of a ... HOTEL BREAK-
FAST, YUM YUM.

Camps for holistic families

Mum's organised four camps for subscribers of The Mother magazine. The first three were held here in Cumbria, one on our land,
and the other two not far from there. The last one was held in North
Yorkshire. There's a lot of work involved behind the scenes. We help
mum with different things before and during camp. Bethany and I
helped to prepare meals and serve food for more than fifty families. We really love the people (adults and children) that we meet
at camp. And I made some really good friends there. It's one of the
highlights of the year to be with so many really lovely families at
one time.

Birthday girl

I've cleverly started a trend by making sure we go away and do
something special for my birthdays. I'm an Aquarian. This started
a couple of years ago when Mum was doing a talk in Bristol for the
launch of one of her books. We stayed with our lovely friends Anton,
Alex, Hugo and Naomi. They made my birthday *very* special. Alex
made chocolate muffins, for a birthday cake. While we were there
we went to a fashion museum, the abbey at Bath, ate at Demuth's
vegetarian café, and had a really lovely time staying with them.

Last year, we were closer to home, and stayed at a vegan B&B in
the Lake District; and then the next day, we went across to Yorkshire
to see the land the magazine camp was going to be held on.

We've just been to Ireland again ~ for my 12th birthday!

Protesting

Not all of our trips away involve pleasure. In 2008, we travelled
to London and back in one day (it ended up being about 10 hours

Portrait of a lady, by Eliza

of train travel) to protest outside parliament against the stupid law which puts the pressure on breastfeeding mums, rather than the property owners concerned, to make sure they're within the law. It's silly, and caused a lot of confusion with some people thinking that babies over six months of age weren't going to be allowed to breastfeed in public.

Places we've explored near our home

We live in a very beautiful part of England, and have many places right on our doorstep. There are Lacey's caves, Long Meg Druids' Circle, the Eden River, Talkin Tarn, the amazing hills of the Lake District, and all the fields, lanes and woods by our village. By not being in school, we can go anywhere, at any time, if we choose.

School versus unschooling

I chose to go to school because Bethany did, as I thought I'd be lonely without her.

I was in the 'good work' assembly three times for my writing (newspaper reports).

These are what I've found to be the main differences between school and unschooling:

There's no timetable with unschooling. Sometimes I'd like to have everything planned out, but they didn't teach much history in school or do much variety (it was mainly the 1930s to '40s history they were teaching).

I couldn't see my cats when I was at school. The good thing about school, was that we'd always come home to a treat Mum had made, like lemon and coconut muffins. I guess she missed us while we were away!

At school, I saw a lot of people every day (some who I didn't like, and some who I did).

At home, I teach myself. At school, someone else is in charge of your learning, and you don't get to choose what you *want* to learn. The teachers got a bit irritating because they spent most of each lesson getting cross at the naughty boys. It felt like I was always waiting for the lesson to start.

The only language they taught at my school was German. They didn't have variety. At home, you can teach yourself any language you want. When we were much younger, Mum taught us some Aramaic. We've learnt a bit of Italian and French.

I don't feel the teachers really appreciated who I was as a person, but judged me on my work and intelligence.

At home, I can choose what to eat, and when. At school, my lunch was packed (and it was always yummy). I didn't have the option of choice once I'd left home in the mornings, and I had to eat at the same time as dozens of other people, whether I felt like it or not.

The spelling tests were way too easy. It was patronising.

When I was nine, the school judged me to have a reading age of 11 years and 3 months (whatever that means!). I taught myself to read when I was about seven. I found the books that school gave us to read were boring. At home, I can choose my reading, and I can read whenever I like. I've got many books on my bookshelf, mostly bought from Bluebell bookshop in our town, some from charity shops and second hand bookshops; and I borrow books from the library.

Headaches: I'm sensitive to things in my environment ~ like lack of fresh air, bright lights, high volume levels and people arguing. I came home from school almost every day with a pounding headache. Lunchtimes were quite difficult because of all the noise in the food hall. Fluorescent lights were used throughout the school, and they were too bright to be under for long.

Everything that was taught in school, I mostly knew anyway ~ so it felt like repeating things over and over. I don't like repetition. Because I tend to have a photographic memory, I need only read something once for it to stick in my head.

Not much artwork was done at school. At home, I can draw and paint all day if I like, and I often do. Mum's filing cabinet is full of my paintings, and some of my work hangs on the walls. She still has the first picture I ever painted when I was a baby. At school, they were more interested in us learning about magnets than being creative in the arts. I never saw the point of magnets!

Every Wednesday at school, there was group singing, but the trouble was you never really got to hear anything because it was all jumbled. At home, I can sing all the time. I particularly like to sing when I'm cooking. I think they go hand in hand. My favourite pieces to sing are in the country music range. Sometimes Dad pulls out his amplifier, and I use the microphone. Dad's a professional singer, so he's able to give me tips. I'm too independent to be told how to do something, so I just tend to do things my own way.

Eliza and her horse companion, Mystery.
Below: Eliza at Earthsong, 2003, before we planted the
orchard.

Eliza at Torquay, Devon. December, 2009.
Below: At eight days old.

I was really good at maths, but I don't enjoy it. I find it boring. At home, I don't have to do maths at all, though Dad encourages me to try a bit from time to time so that when I leave home I can understand enough to get by in the world.

Literacy was done most days at school. We had to focus on a theme, like the environment, and then did writing based on that. I enjoy reading and writing, but found the way that it was presented to be very boring.

At home, you don't have to wear uniforms. School requires uniforms so everybody looks the same. I guess it's to make children like sheep so they can be herded up, if necessary. I prefer to choose my own clothes for the day. Some days, I stay in my pyjamas until lunchtime. Other days, I might change my clothes a couple of times, depending on my mood.

The handwriting lessons were a time of being judged. My handwriting is different because I'm left handed, and I don't feel the teachers really take this into account. At home, we're not judged by our writing, however now that Bethany's studying graphology, I'm trying to be a bit neater!

At lunch time, there were people paid to come and supervise the children. One of the ladies was just lovely. We got on well. She'd had a water birth and was vegetarian, so I feel we had some things in common. The other supervisor was rather mean and didn't have a pleasant personality. At home, we don't have to be supervised while we eat or play! We're trusted to do what we need or want to do. Our parents don't expect us to get into trouble.

The school bus trip (eight miles a day) always gave me a headache. There was a stupid rule that said that only the year sixes could sit up the back. We had a really nice lady who was a bus monitor to ensure good behaviour. No school bus trips are needed with unschooling! We do travel on trains though, sometimes, like if we're going to London. That's usually fun because Bethany and I get to walk around and tell the people who are going to the toilet that the loo's not working. It's a long way to London without a wee stop. (Laughing)

One of my passions is cooking. I love reading recipe books, eating, going to cafés and trying new food, and photographing food. I would never have had the opportunity to put so many hours into this hobby if I was in school five days a week. We didn't even get to cook much in school! We did make a sandwich one day! *Boring!*

Eliza doing saxophone practice. Opposite: petting donkeys in the snow.

What's the point? In year five, we had to make a vegetable pie. It was BLAND. I don't think they'd ever heard of seasonings. At home, we eat all types of food, and I'm used to different herbs and spices, and cuisine from cultures around the world. I don't enjoy the texture of mushrooms (but I like the flavour), and I don't eat avocados, but other than that I tend to eat all the vegetables and fruits we have.

It's always exciting to me when we explore new cafés and restaurants. There aren't many places in Cumbria that serve good vegan or vegetarian wholefoods, so these treats tend to be when we leave the county. The last great meals I had away from home were at Wagamama when we were in Manchester and Dublin. They were noodle dishes in a spicy sauce, with tofu. The flavours were amazing!

I prefer unschooling and being at home, to being in school.

Part Four
by Veronika Sophia Robinson

Summer

Our favourite summer in England: 2003. Hot, hot, hot! Every other Summer, in terms of hot weather, has proved disappointingly conspicuous by its absence. We keep waiting for the thermostat to go up, but all it does is rain and stay too temperate for our tastes. One Summer, my Mum visited from Australia, and sat in a ski suit by the fire in July! Each Summer, we anticipate an abundance of vegetables and fruits from the garden, and live in eternal hope that the Sun will shine brightly and warmly.

A nettle a day keeps the iron tablets away

Nettle tea is so good for the body, and is refreshing. High in iron, it's well worth having a stash of dried leaves in your kitchen. You can make it from fresh leaves, too. Nettles lose their sting as soon as heat is applied to the leaves.

I often use freshly picked leaves in my vegetable juices so I can get the maximum nourishment from this incredible 'weed'. Nettles are deliberately left to grow in our garden, if not for our own use, then for the wildlife which visit. Nettles are always an indication of beautifully fertile soil, so adore them and let the plants flourish.

Eliza's nettle soup
Large bunch/es of nettles
5 potatoes, chopped into small cubes
2 onions
5 cups of water
Vegetable bouillon (yeast-free)

Gently fry the onions until clear, and then add the potatoes. We don't peel the skin off potatoes as we use organically grown ones. There's no need to wash the nettles if they've grown away from roadside pollution. Cut with scissors, and add to the pot. Cover with five cups of boiling water which has had 5 tablespoons of bouillon added, and simmer until the potatoes are soft. You can blend a little of the soup, and return it to the pot to make it creamier. Season with freshly ground black pepper, if desired.

Foraging for gooseberries and raspberries

Since the girls were toddlers, we'd go walking the lanes looking for fruits to forage, such as gooseberries and raspberries. They can take you to every bush, tree and cane for miles around, including cherry trees and elderberries. Even within the confines of our garden, they'll stand for hours picking blackcurrants, and popping them (sugar-free!) straight into their mouths. They never seem to tire of this natural way of eating. As a mother, I feel such joy that they eat these tiny, tart berries that are bursting with vitamin C. It's such a good boost to their immune systems. The garden also features strawberries and blueberries, not that Paul or I get much of a look in!

One Summer, I decided to make a load of Elderflower Champagne as a birthday present for my husband. Lovely idea, but all the bottles exploded! I was more disappointed that the hand-made labels were ruined. Now we make elderflower cordial instead, using the delicately- scented flowers soaked in spring water and agave syrup. It's lovely!

Elderflower is used homeopathically to treat fevers. Due to its high vitamin C content, it's used for bronchitis, colds and coughs. Avoid adding sugar, though, as it strips minerals and vitamins from the body. Opt for a sweetener like agave, which doesn't affect blood sugar levels or rot teeth. To bring on sweating (feverish colds), make an infusion of 2 t flowers in 1 cup of boiling water. Leave for ten minutes and drink hot.

Raspberry leaf tea is perfect for pregnant women, but is good for anyone, especially those who are recovering from illness. We dry the leaves, and sometimes the berries, to make tea. Like nettles, these leaves are also rich in iron, which is invaluable for anyone who wishes to build up their iron stores.

Wild Swimming

We live walking and cycling distance from an open air swimming pool in the next village. A season's pass is invaluable when the weather's fine, as it means the girls can go there every day of the week for as long as they like. Often they'll choose to go after school hours to catch up with children they know, but they're just as likely to want to go during school time so they can enjoy the peace of the pool to themselves. One thing that's quite common amongst unschoolers is the desire to use public facilities during school hours so they're not so noisy!

Living rurally means the girls have the chance to swim in natural waterways, like the beck down the road, the edge of the Eden river, or a tarn in the mountains of the Lake District. Life without school means that you can do all sorts of activities when you feel like it, rather than when you're allowed to do them.

Below: The Eden River, at Lazonby Bridge, photographed by Eliza.

Gardening

My great love of Summer is being able to be in the garden, whether it's having my fingers deep in the soil, or sitting back with a freshly made vegetable juice while listening to birdsong and gazing upon the Pennines. Our unschooling life is based in the garden during this time of the year. The girls drag their books, drawings, instruments and other goodies outside, and set up an activity area to last the day. Sometimes they'll be lying on rugs beneath the plum tree, or up in the sunshine playing chase with the cats. Eliza camps out in the living willow house we've grown, and reads for hour upon hour in her shady, private den. As Paul and I work from home, it means we can enjoy being outside with the girls during sunny times as well.

Throughout Summer, we eat our meals in the garden. It seems pointless sitting inside four walls when we can eat our food to the sound of birds, sheep, cows, bees, and the smells of honeysuckle, fennel and fresh air. Our eyes can rest upon the fields, which rise up to meet the Pennines. All our senses are nurtured and nourished. Many school children don't get to sit down with their family to eat meals, but instead have ready-made TV meals to gulp down unconsciously while watching television, or playing computer games ~ or both at once!

There's something very connecting and enlivening about eating one's meal amongst the vegetable gardens where the produce has been grown and nurtured.

Green Goddess Dressing

1 tablespoon fresh parsley, finely chopped
2 green onions
1 clove garlic
1/4 cup water
1/2 pound silky tofu
1 tablespoon cider vinegar
2 teaspoons tamari
1 tablespoon tahini
1/2 teaspoon vegan bouillon

Mix all ingredients in a blender until smooth and silky. Serve in a jug, and pour over dark, leafy greens when ready to eat.

Eliza's home-made lemonade

Summertime and home-made lemonade, under the shade of the plum tree, go hand in hand.

5 organic lemons
1 organic lime
3 litres of spring water
Half a cup of agave syrup

Remove seeds where possible, and most of the peel. Keep some zest, and include it with the fruits (but only if using organic), water and syrup, and blend on high speed. Chill before serving, and had a sprig of home-grown, fresh peppermint.

Oat and Cinnamon Cookies
By Eliza

4 cups oats
¼ cup sesame seeds
1 cup dates, chopped
½ cup pumpkin seeds
80g agave syrup
½ cup sunflower seeds
¼ cup brown rice syrup
½ cup tahini
Pinch cinnamon
½ cup carob or cacao
150ml light olive oil
250g good quality margarine
½ cup rye flour

Mix margarine with flour, oats and agave. Then add the other ingredients, and when well mixed, make into small biscuits, about five centimetres wide. Bake for 20 minutes at 170 degrees Celsius. Allow to cool before serving.

Watercress

Watercress is rich in zinc, and therefore an excellent plant to include in your diet if you're planning to conceive. It flowers in the Summer, and grows in clear streams, ponds, ditches, and at the site of springs. It was traditionally used to treat TB, and is high in vitamin C and iodine. In our family, we use it as a tasty addition to salads and soups.

Bay and Onion soup

With all the yummy fruits and vegetables which are available in Summer, it might seem odd to have soup then, but this one is so delicious we eat it all year round, but especially when there are plenty of spuds and onions in the garden. Our bay leaf tree supplies us with leaves at any time of the year. You can dry the leaves for storage, or use them fresh from the tree.

Serves family of four

2 bay leaves
2 large onions, finely chopped
1 potato, chopped
4 T olive oil
1 litre of unsweetened and unflavoured rice or soya milk.
300 ml vegetable bouillon
Freshly ground black pepper
Maldon sea salt, if desired

Sauté onions until clear, then add the remaining ingredients, and simmer until the potatoes are soft. Remove the bay leaf, and blend half the soup. Add it back to the pot, and adjust seasonings, if necessary. Beware, this is one of those soups that you just keep going back for.

Picnics

Summer is a time that calls for us to picnic at every opportunity. By the river, the tarn, at the caves, up a hill, in a park...every day's a good day for a picnic. If the weather turns out to be dour, we pull out a blanket on the lounge room floor, and tell stories or play Scrabble. "Breaking bread" is an age-old way to socialise and become intimate with friends and family. Given the intimacy involved in being an unschooled family, it's no surprise that mealtimes are a major feature of how, when, and where we socialise with each other.

Horse riding

I grew up on the back of a horse, or several dozen horse backs, actually. The smell of horse sweat, and even manure, is pleasantly attractive to me. My childhood would have been wonderful if horse riding wasn't limited to after school or weekends. My joys were found in grooming down a horse, and riding up by the creek, ducking under the branches of eucalyptus trees, and disappearing up the mountains ~ just me and my equine friend. It helped me forge a sense of independence, adventure and solitude.

The Summer before last, Eliza went horse riding each week with a teenage girl in the village. She learnt to groom the horse, as well as ride. Her confidence grew as she overcame the various fears associated with getting on a horse's back...and coming off it! Eliza adores animals (except for rats down the bottom of the garden near the farmer's barns, or that get dragged in by the cats!), and really valued her time getting to know Mystery and Swallow better. The horses' owner now works, and is studying full-time, so riding with her isn't an option at the moment; but we still walk up and see the horses whenever we're up that side of the village.

Spontaneous Learning
Autumn, 2003 ~ The Mother magazine, Issue Seven

These gorgeous Autumnal mornings have a chill that nips at my ankles when I climb from our warm, cosy bed. I'm acutely aware that I've been riding the high of a glorious Summer, and now it's disappearing quickly. A slight panic comes over me when I realise this page is still blank. What have I/we to show for these past three months? Granted, Summer is actually school holiday time, and I could get away with leaving it blank, but the backbone of unschooling is that *life* is an education ~ so I don't get time off for good behaviour.

So what have we to share apart from our golden suntans? Are we wiser? Learning well? Healthier? Richer? More loving? How do I measure such things? I don't use the National Curriculum or daily writing books as yardsticks to measure how clever my kids are. Their true worth and value can only be measured internally, by themselves. We don't keep shelves or boxes full of work to see if we're 'improving'; or gold stars; give grades.

For most people who choose the unschooling path, the most detested question is 'What about socialisation?' Personally, that one doesn't wind me up half as much as 'Have you done your lessons today?' As I always say, if I'd wanted them to do lessons they'd have been in school years ago.

The very foundation of unschooling is based on the idea that the more you leave children to learn on their own, the more they do learn. And they learn precisely because their natural curiosity is not impeded by an adult. They learn through feeling, asking, exploring, examining. Learning can happen at any time, but it can't be boxed into a time frame.

So how could I possibly measure a million moments of spontaneous learning in this web we call life? If someone were to see my five year old daughter playing in the vegetable gardens with a trowel while I was digging nearby, they'd be wrong to think she wasn't learning.

Chances are that Eliza will be leading a discussion on geography, asking, for example, which country she'll get to when she digs to the other side of the Earth. Has anyone been there? Have I ever been there? Why not? And then she asks if other planets have countries on them. This kind of questioning is normal for unschooled children. It takes an enormous amount of patience on my part to keep up with it. I fail miserably at times. However, they still get 1,000 more questions answered than if they were in an institutional setting. It's worth remembering that in terms of humanity's history, schooling is a relatively recent phenomenon. How did children learn about life and the world around them before schools were invented? They asked questions!

During the heatwave in Summer, the girls were playing in a field by my feet as I shovelled road plainings into a wheelbarrow to place on the right of way to our land. It was hot, and it was taking a long time. You can count on Eliza to turn every situation into an examination of mathematical equations. "How long would it take to lay this road if we had two adults helping you?" "What if it wasn't so hot, and we had two wheelbarrows, and five people helping you?" "How about if we asked a farmer to do it with his tractor?" You get the picture!

I never take it for granted that my girls are fortunate enough to be able to pull up a bunch of carrots, or grab a handful of peas or pick themselves a cucumber. We entrusted seeds into Mother Earth, and allowed them space and time to grow. Is this not a metaphor for their childhood, indeed, for any creative project in life?

We learn to develop patience. To wait, wait, wait ~ and look! There's a tiny green shoot pushing: pushing hard through the soil to reach the light. And, yes! Two green leaves. Weeks later, this same plant is unrecognisable. And a month later, we're tying it to bamboo canes as it imitates Jack's famous beanstalk. And then there are the first flowers; and finally, the green beans appear. Can the girls wait? Wait another week so the beans are longer than their little fingers? Not likely… "Just one, Mum? Please?"

Some children have never seen vegetables growing, and some have never eaten fresh vegetables on the same day they were picked. And sadly, some children don't know where vegetables even come from.

What am I preparing my children for? A job? A career? No. Simply to enjoy life, and to know it can be whatever they choose to make of it. The seed is the basis of life. Each day I'm more convinced that they can learn just about everything they'll ever need to know by understanding and working with Nature. The planting of a cucumber seed, which yields dozens more cucumbers a few months later, is a holistic study and experience of maths, geography, biology, ag-

The Dance Of The Moonlight Water Nymphs

Bethany Angelika Robinson

Bethany's composition for grade four violin, with Trinity College.

riculture, economics, food studies, science, and most importantly of all: gratitude.

We also learn to spell, and write stories, from this experience. And dare I say it, it's even possible to have a social experience because of a vegetable. Imagine that: home educated children actually having a social experience! Who'd have thought? Unschooling doesn't mean living in denial or living like a hermit. Vegetables are great to give to your friends, to neighbours, and even strangers. As for our pumpkins, they've impacted our local bookshop, in the children's section, for an Autumn celebration. With this will come the fun of a storytime with lots of other children. They'll share soup made from our organic pumpkins, and hear children's author Helen Cooper read from her book.

The worlds between Summer and Winter seem somehow bigger when your child's education is home based. By the very nature of the seasons, we'll inevitably spend the majority of our time inside during Winter ~ the complete opposite to Summer.

We'll use some creative genius to bring Nature indoors for the worst weathered days. I'm hoping we can keep up a good dose of sunlight by spending time in our newly erected polytunnel ~ reading, chatting, digging.

It takes energy to deal with cabin fever and children 24/7. Spontaneity and planning have to be rolled into one. Our days will have a lot more planned activity, such as swimming, and having friends to lunch. I'm looking forward to time by the fireside with my girls, wonderful books, piano playing, singing, and the company of friends.

After months of spending most of our days outdoors, it will be vital that we keep up with the long, daily walks. It's one of the activities I most enjoy doing with the girls. There's so much to see, hear, smell, touch and talk about. It does, however, mean I'll have nonstop questions rolling my way. Now, where were those ear muffs?

Paul's Birthday

Paul's birthday is our only Summer one, so we have to make sure he has plenty of good food memories to get him through till the next family birthday. His cake of choice is always chocolate. Breakfast is cooked: tofu, tomatoes and mushrooms. His evening meal is home-made curry. We used to get Indian take-away as a special birthday treat until we realised that our curry was better than the ones we bought.

Chocolate Blueberry Cake
By Eliza

½ cup chocolate (or carob if you prefer, as it's caffeine-free)
3 cups flour (gluten free works beautifully with this recipe)
1 cup agave syrup
1 t salt
2 t baking powder
150ml sunflower oil
2 cups water
2 T apple cider vinegar
1 tub blueberries
½ cup sugar-free blueberry jam

Mix together the chocolate, flour, salt, baking powder and agave. Add the rest of the ingredients (except the blueberries and jam). Mix well, and pour into two small tins, or one large one if you don't want layers. Bake at 180C for half an hour.

When the cakes are cool, spread the jam in between them, then top with blueberries before sandwiching it with the top layer of cake.

Paul's favourite curry

This will feed two families, so invite someone over to celebrate with you!

2 onions
5 potatoes
head of broccoli
5 carrots
handful of green beans
2 cups peas
2 red peppers
1 aubergine
2 packs of tofu
2 cups sultanas
two tubes tomato puree (optional)
3 tins coconut milk
5 litres of bouillon
curry powder
bay leaves
black pepper
coconut oil or sunflower oil

Chop all the vegetables into bite sized pieces, except the onions, which should be finely chopped. Sauté the onions in coconut oil (or sunflower), then add 3 - 4 (more depending on taste) tablespoons of good quality curry powder, and gently fry. Do not brown or burn or you'll have to start again. Add potatoes and carrots, and gently fry. Add aubergines and bay leaves, and make sure all vegetables have been coated in curry and oil. Add enough boiling water/bouillon to just cover the vegetables, and boil until the potatoes are almost cooked, then add the other vegetables, and sultanas. (Alternatively, steam the vegetables lightly before adding to the curry). Cook for a few minutes, then add the coconut milk, tomato puree (optional), tofu cubes and black pepper.

Allow everything to cook through, and serve with basmati rice or quinoa.

Food from the garden

Without question, one of Summer's highlights is that every evening meal is picked from the garden. There's always an abundance of greenery: rocket, mizuna, pak choi, cos lettuce, red battavia, chicory, spinach, red chard. These form the basis of whatever we eat. The herb garden is in full growth now, so we can pick plenty of aromatic leaves from there, too.

So many children have a disconnection from the food they eat. My girls have grown up with a garden that feeds them, and have planted seeds themselves. Like me, they feel such joy and excitement as the first seeds emerge. Cumbria's Winters are a challenge, though, with food being limited to root vegetables, red and green cabbages, Brussels sprouts, celery, celeriac and a few greens like claytonia and pak choi (till the heavy frosts).

The girls have learnt about biodynamic gardening, and how to plant, tend and harvest according to the Moon. We plant leafy vegetables during the times when the Moon is in water signs: Pisces, Cancer and Scorpio. Our root vegetables are planted, tended (hoeing, weeding) and harvested during the Earth signs of Capricorn, Virgo and Taurus. When the Moon is in the fire signs of Aries, Leo or Sagittarius we plant 'fruits', which include vegetables such as beans, peas, pumpkins, corn ~ anything where you pick off a 'fruit', rather than a leaf or root. Our flowers are all planted during the Moon's transit through air signs: Libra, Aquarius and Gemini. We've experimented many times using the same batch of seeds planted on consecutive days, in the same growing conditions, but in different Moon signs ~ and the results are extraordinary. Many commercial biodynamic farmers tend to just plant when the weather's good, and not according to the Moon, which is such a shame as the cosmic forces are vital during the corresponding times.

The day after Paul's 51st birthday, in late Summer, with Bethany, aged three and a half, in the back garden, Glassonby, Cumbria.

Solstice

The day with the longest number of light hours arrives. Will we be able to sleep when the sky is so bright? The backpack is filled with picnic food, and off we walk to Long Meg and her Daughters' Druid Circle. It's usually really busy there at this time of the year, but if we go early enough we'll beat the tourists. We cut through the churchyard, horse field, farmer's field, woodland, and by the back of the raspberry farm ~ and then we're there. I spent many nights of my childhood sleeping beneath the starry southern hemisphere skies, and knew the constellations intimately. I still haven't adjusted to (or learnt!) the northern constellations, but I do so love to watch the night sky. At the Summer Solstice, it seems as if the stars will never come out to twinkle, but they always do ~ if even for just a few hours. And then, ever so quickly, the days start disappearing again ~ shorter, shorter, shorter.

Angelikah, with her granddaughters, Bethany and Eliza, at Long Meg Stone Circle, Glassonby, Cumbria.

Starflower salad

Both the cucumber-tasting leaves and the pretty blue flowers of starflower can be used in salads. Try adding some nasturtiums, too, as the blue and orange look spectacular together.

Starflower grows so easily, that it's such a shame not to put a few seeds in your garden. They'll come back year after year.

The chamomile field

One of my favourite things is to walk, barefooted, amongst chamomile flowers, and wait for the apple-like scent to release from the beautiful daisy-style flowers. The magnificence of Summer is amplified by such treasured moments. In the photo above, my mother is playing music to her granddaughters while they enjoy the scent of the chamomile field. A friend said to me that it was this photo that convinced her to home educate her children, because it captured something very beautiful.

Throughout childhood, my mother often made chamomile tea to help soothe me. I smile to myself now that Eliza often asks for a chamomile tea when she needs to wind down a bit after we've been out to town.

This herb is used to stimulate the appetite, as well as to calm digestion. The tea can relieve nausea. Chamomile makes a great poultice for wounds, and is useful to add fresh to baths, and for a hair wash. We love it as a tea, especially before bedtime.

You can buy chamomile tea, but it's lovelier to harvest your own flowers. Dry them somewhere dark, and store them in a dry container. Simply add a spoon or two of the flowers to a cup of boiling water. Leave to infuse for a few minutes before drinking.

The Summer Altar

Summer gifts us with such an abundance of wildflowers that really brighten up the home, and remind us of all the beauty that exists in our lives.

Sunflowers or starflowers?

In the Summer, our garden features, amongst other things, sunflowers and starflowers (borage). Along with beautifully scented freesias, they're my favourite flowers, and yet they're so very different from each other. Sunflowers are big and showy. They shout out to you "Here I am! Look at me!" Mine grow 15 to 20 feet, easily, towering well above the other flowers, herbs and vegetables. I use the seeds from my wholefood order, as they're of a variety designed to grow strong and well, and to produce big heads for commercial harvesting. They're such a delight to me.

Starflowers, on the other hand, are so delicate and dainty. Their fragile, tiny star-shaped flowers press beautifully between the pages of my diary, and get posted out with cards: my Summer's keepsake.

Starflower is my tea of choice if I feel a cold or cough coming on. It's brilliant for all sorts of ailments. It's a herb that should be in every holistic family's natural medicine basket. It increases the quantity and quality of breast milk in a lactating mother, and is also recommended for easing pre-menstrual tension, as well as helping menopausal women by supporting the adrenal glands in oestrogen production. It's useful for healing from adrenal fatigue, too.

Holistic parents use starflower for clearing the eruptive diseases of childhood, such as measles and chickenpox; for flu, coughs and feverish colds. It has an expectorant action on the respiratory system, is a decongestant, and is excellent for catarrh, chest infections and sore throats. Starflower is useful for any irritation or soreness of the chest or throat. It also has the same expectorant action on the urinary and digestive systems (making it useful for IBS and gastritis). It's a relaxant.

Starflower is well-known for helping people through grief and sadness.

This cleansing herb helps to detoxify the body by increasing sweat, and acting as a diuretic. It's particularly helpful for skin problems (rashes, boils, eczema, psoriasis, etc.), and for asthma, bronchitis, rheumatism and arthritis. It stimulates the adrenal glands, and helps to counter the effects of steroids. Known since ancient times as being a heart tonic, starflower calms and soothes heart palpitations, and relaxes during times of sickness.

Starflower grows annually, and thrives in 'waste' places, such as wreckage yards. The original name for this herb was Llanwenlys (Welsh) or Burrage (Borage), which means herb of gladness. Even in ancient times, starflower had quite a reputation for fostering courage, and easing melancholy. Bees love this plant, and it's often nicknamed Bee's Bread. The plant itself only grows about 1½ feet high, though it grows about 3 feet wide. It's a companion plant to strawberries, and looks beautiful amongst other flowers.

Starflowers don't jump up and down like sunflowers, but as you can see, they're vital, powerful, and a plant to definitely have in your garden.

I grow sunflowers and starflowers side by side. Bees and butterflies don't play favourites, and nor should we. In our culture, the kudos is on 'big and showy'. Most children these days want to grow up and 'be a celebrity'. There seems to be very little education or role modelling about what fame actually means.

Yes, encourage your children to make their mark in this world; to stand strong, be bold and upfront like a sunflower, if they wish, but whatever they do, encourage them to develop integrity, and always include that as their bright and beautiful gift to this world. Sunflowers and starflowers both have their parts to play in the garden of life: and both are beautiful.

Part Five

Bethany at one year old. Auckland, New Zealand.

My Chapter
by Bethany A. Robinson

Bethany and Veronika, Summer 1996, Auckland, New Zealand.

I live in Cumbria, England, with my Dad, Paul, Mum, Veronika, sister, Eliza, and two mischievous cats, Grenzy and William.

I've been home-educated since birth, but I went to primary school for a term and a half, and secondary school for half a term.

The following is divided into sections according to topic:

Writing and Reading

As I write this, I sit on my bed listening to one of my favourite bands, *Muse*. This activity is a daily event. I don't have a set time of day; I just get on with it. Just because I'm on my bed, it doesn't mean I'm not doing anything constructive: open on my lap lies a black, hard-cover book, with two dolphin stickers on the cover. Said book is filled with poems, plays, songs, monologues, or whatever I've been inspired to write.

I love writing.

I went to a youth playwrights' course at a nearby theatre. It was really good, and I learned a lot about writing plays, and about writing in general. I also learned how to "put my thoughts onto paper", which should be easy: but it's not, for me.

When I was writing during the playwrights' course, my mind worked best when I was listening to music. Generally, *Evanescence* (an American rock band) worked best: their lyrics inspired me.

After a while, I began to find writing plays hard: I had to fit the entire story into a fixed period of time, and it was starting to feel, oddly, wrong.

So I started to write the story in small sections, then fitting it together ~ like a soap opera.

Then I made the mistake of writing songs. It sounds innocent enough, doesn't it? But it was easier than I expected. And now, if I begin to write a song, I can't stop, and I write about three at once.

I adore reading. Once I start a good book, I'm sucked into its many pages, and can barely return to the normal ways of life. When I was about ten or eleven, I enjoyed the His Dark Materials series, and most other books of a similar genre. I liked the Harry Potters, too, and still do.

From the ages of, roughly, ten to eleven or twelve, I liked all of the Jacqueline Wilson-Jean Ure-Cathy Cassidy style books, which all seemed to feature thirteen-year-old girls. However, now that I *am* thirteen, I'm not so sure about them. It's so hard to say "This is my favourite book of all time", and honestly mean it. About three or four months ago, I almost certainly would have said "The Twilight Saga". I still don't quite know what my favourite book is, but I recently read Dead Until Dark, by Charlaine Harris, and thoroughly enjoyed it.

I volunteered at my local library last Summer, for the annual Summer Reading Challenge, or The Quest Seekers, as the library calls it. I volunteered a total of twenty hours. I would have liked to have done more, but ~ as I'm only thirteen ~ I was restricted to only twenty hours.

The job entailed helping children – of ages five to twelve – discover new books and authors, and discuss their progress in the Reading Challenge. In doing so, I boosted my confidence, and enjoyed working with other people who loved books as much as I do.

I would like to do some voluntary work for a good charity/good cause, in the future; maybe something involving animals, because I want to do something worthwhile, that helps others. Animals, especially, for they don't have a voice, and cannot stand up for their rights.

Music
My first instrument is piano, but I also play violin. I started playing the piano when I was eight, five years ago, and then the violin one year later. I play the violin in the Cumbria Youth Training Orchestra (CYTO).

I've never achieved a distinction in a violin exam, I'm sorry to say, but I got a merit for grade one, and missed distinction by a couple of marks for grades two, three and four. However, I passed my piano grades one and three with distinction, and missed it for grade two by three marks.

Recently, I purchased a guitar, and I am thoroughly enjoying learning to play it.

A year or so ago, I was lying in bed, trying desperately to go back to sleep. It was Winter - not far from Christmas - and I was dreading getting out of bed to face the cold world surrounding me.

Suddenly, Eliza – full of energy – came a hop-skip-jumping into our bedroom.

I snuggled under my duvet, faking sleep, but Eliza knew me too well, and plopped herself noisily onto my bed.

ELIZA: Guess what!

ME: (Groan).

ELIZA: There's a big parcel under Mum's bed!

ME: (Groan).

Eliza ran out of the room, excitedly, into Mum and Dad's room.

Oh, dear; if I knew Eliza ~ which I did ~ she would come a-yelling at the top of her voice to say what the present was.

I heard the crumple of torn paper, the gasp of awe, and the loud thump-thump of Eliza running across the wooden floor.

ELIZA: It's a ... !

I covered my ears, but not quickly enough. I had known all along that it was a flute (Mum had been meaning to call my aunt who had offered it to me: it used to belong to my cousin), but I didn't want to spoil it for Mum.

I heard the last bit:

ELIZA: Flute!

I sat up, and hissed:

ME: Don't let Mum know that you know!

ELIZA: But aren't you happy?

ME: I'd rather have waited till Mum gave it to me! Go and tell Mum what you did, and don't miss anything out!

ELIZA: No!

ME: Wait, yeah, don't. Act as if it never happened. Don't spoil it for her.

Eliza must have felt guilty, and ~ talk about reverse psychology ~ started down stairs.

ME: No! Don't do this!

Eliza left the room.

I listened to Eliza's tearful confession in horror, wondering how on Earth I could have prevented it. Mum bought the house down, and not through laughter ~ it took her a few minutes to see the funny side. So now I have a flute!

I didn't much like the fact that at school we only had music once a week . . .

School

... And maths practically every day.

Our Maths teacher didn't even care enough about our education to check our answers. She wrote the answers on the whiteboard, and we were told to "tick or cross" our answers. So, of course, us bored eleven-year-olds all corrected our wrong answers, ticked them, and got top marks.

Then there was Science; I never did quite work out what the periodic table was, while in school.

The two Science teachers were of very different species. My favourite was Australian. She called chickens "chooks"; she was very fair, and, by far, one of the nicest teachers in the school. And because the school principal thought that I was intelligent ~ apparently ~ I was put in "Year 7, 1", rather than "Year 7, 2"; "Year 7, 1" was apparently for the intelligent pupils. I, however, believe that the pre-teens in "Year 7, 2" were just as smart as the others . . .

But I was a mere eleven-year-old girl: I couldn't have my say.

"Year 7, 2" had the nice teacher: I had Mrs MaCDonald ~ Or Old MaCDonald, as we called her behind her back.

We used to sing:
Miss MaCDonald had a school,
E I E I O,
And in that school she held some kids
Ca-a-a-aptive.

The boys were somewhat better off: they all wore their ties the traditional way, small knot at the top, and the rest hanging stiffly. Us girls copied the Year Nine girls, (one of whom I would now be, if still in school): they wore their ties loose, and fat at the top, and short and stiff at the bottom.

Old MaCDonald would stroll casually along the corridor, and without a word, would "fix" our ties. If in a bad mood (frequently), she would keep us in at break times for "sloppy" uniforms. Our pain was self-inflicted, I suppose, but still . . . If one pupil came into the classroom late and so much as said "Hi" to a friend, then they, and the rest of the class, would lose their precious fifteen minutes of break time.

What was the point of uniforms, anyway? Besides breaking the bank, that is. They're meant to be "equalisers", but they just make children into sheep. And any daring pupil brave enough to attempt the crime of defying uniform customisation, would have to sacrifice

Dancing the Cha Cha Cha, illustrated by Bethany.

Bethany at Forest Row, Sussex aged 11; Autumn on the village green, aged 13; Bethany trying to outrace the gale force winds on the beach, Devon, December 2009; The Big Freeze, Glassonby, Cumbria, January 2010.

their quarter of an hour's freedom. Even just for a sequined, black ~ the school colour ~ headband, one of my friends was the opposite of a teacher's pet all week.

Then there was the Food Tech teacher. She was a strange creature.

On our week-long induction to the school, one of our subjects was Food Technology (cooking). We made pink fairy cakes, which was kind of fun. But when we returned in the new school year, as year sevens, the teacher had us learning to cut apples. Cutting apples! Why in that order? And why so basic? We were eleven, not five. My younger sister could cook a full on meal, unsupervised, by the time she was nine. Two weeks later, once we'd mastered the complicated art of cutting apples, we were on to Health and Safety in the Kitchen. We'd all learned that either at home or in primary school.

Then when our teacher was off sick, our supply teacher asked what we'd been learning. We said "Health and Safety in the Kitchen". He said that we should have learned all of that ages ago. We said that we had. He told us to draw our favourite food. For the duration of the hour long lesson. Our Art teacher could have done that.

The school garden was pretty plain. "Pretty" is pretty ironic. The garden was a small patch of muddy grass, with a tennis court at the side that, may I add, was of no use to me whatsoever. Secondary schools are supposed to welcome newcomers, and make them feel at home, are they not? Possibly not. My school didn't even have a garden bench.

Sometimes, I wish I could go back to school, but only for a day, not on a permanent basis. I could stand up to the teachers, and make amends for all of the eleven-year-old, shy, behaviour.

HOME-EDUCATION

I have the following divided into small sections. They are all things about my childhood that I fondly remember, such as smells, sounds, or simply, happy memories.

Tomato Leaves

In a polytunnel at Earthsong (a small field that we used to own), Mum grew tomato plants. I loved the smell of the leaves more than I loved the tomatoes. Recently, I smelled a familiar smell in the garden. In one sense I knew what it was, but I still couldn't quite place it. And then I realised: it was a tomato plant! I barely noticed that there was a small tomato growing red, on the plant, because that smell was so familiar, and I loved it so much.

String orchestra tune up

Some people, understandably, may find the sound of a string orchestra ~ or any orchestra, for that matter ~ annoying and ear-splitting. I, however, feel safe and comforted when I'm sitting half way along the line of violin players, tuning. I don't know why. My friends from the orchestra would probably think I had hearing issues, and wonder how on Earth I could like such a sound. I suppose it's an acquired taste ~ or sound, perhaps. Maybe it's just a familiar sound.

Apple-juiced red cabbage

As our family tradition, at Christmas, we have roast vegetables, a nut/seed roast and stir-fried red cabbage, with nutmeg and apple juice. I love all of it, but I especially love the cabbage: strangely, because I hate cabbage. Not this way, though. When someone says "Christmas dinner" to me, I think of stir-fried red cabbage, with nutmeg and apple juice.

My back garden

The back garden ~ and the front garden ~ of The Cottage, I think, are beautiful...in a Veronika Robinson sort of way. To simplify, it looks like a jungle. Not just any old jungle, though: it is filled with sunflowers, fuchsias, starflowers (borage, to some) fennel, and lots more. It's not a traditional garden, but it's beautiful. And it's much better than it was when we first moved here: it was boring, plain, and enough to make anyone move out.

Bethany and Eliza playing their instruments among the Autumn leaves, 2009

My first music lessons

I started piano lessons when I was eight. Some children start a lot earlier, but it seems like a pretty long time ago to me: nearly six years ago. It was nearly half my life ago.

I started violin lessons a year later: five years ago, when I was nine. That seems like a lifetime ago, as well. I could barely hold the bow, unlike now. It's strange to think that once, I couldn't read music: it's part of me now, and I can't imagine my life without it. Actually, I can: it would be a horrible, boring life.

Dad reading to me and Eliza

When Eliza and I were little, Dad would read to us nearly every night. Even if he'd been working all day, he'd read us a children's classic, "The Lion, The Witch and the Wardrobe", or "Pippi Long-stocking" (or something else). He had an individual voice for every single character. Even the girls in "Little Women" had different variations of an American accent. And Aslan (the lion). I didn't know that a human voice could be so low.

Paper crafts

When Eliza and I were little, we made Christmas decorations every year. We made paper dolls, too. I used to want to be an artist, and have a large, neat desk covered with paper, pens, pencils and easels. There was no chance of having a neat desk back then: I wasn't quite as organised as I am now.

Christmas Eve not Christmas Day

It's a German tradition to celebrate Christmas on Christmas Eve, rather than Christmas Day. It may seem like making Christmas shorter, but, in actual fact, it doesn't: we ~ Mum, Eliza and I ~ prepare the Christmas dinner, and play Christmas CDs. Then, in the evening, we eat dinner, and Eliza and I play Christmas carols on our instruments.

Autumn

In the Autumn, the sycamore tree in the centre of the village turns orange ~ and red, brown and beautiful. Throughout our childhood, Mum would take us into the garden or the village to collect Autumn-ish things for an Autumn table (altar), such as maple leaves, acorns, apples and pumpkins. A year or so ago, Eliza found a pair of rollerblades in a local charity shop. Two pairs, actually. They were only £2 each. We had loads of fun rollerblading through the Autumn leaves.

Grandmother, but really a Goddess

Grandmother is perhaps the most fun grandma ever, for lots of reasons. She would take us for long walks, generally to the local church. She would take us inside, and point to one of the seats. There would be licorice, or an apricot flapjack there on the seat. Angelikah said that angels left them there for us. I believed her, then. Once, while walking, we found licorice in a large, pink poppy. She must have walked there especially to put it there, before taking us with her.

The Cats

When I was six, a girl of about twelve, who lived up the road, knocked on the front door with a small, black kitten in her arms. The kitten's mother must have been run over, or something: and her poor baby left homeless. We kept the kitten, and called her Bella. It suited her: she was beautiful.

A year later, she gave birth, under my bed, to a litter of five tiny kittens:

*Athena: Eliza and I decided that she was the eldest. She was tabby, and long haired, like a Persian. Grandmother named her.

*Elvis: the "second", and extremely cute ~ though they all were. Dad named him after Elvis Presley. Our Elvis had a smudge-like white patch on his chin, which made him look mischievous. Every time he walked out through the cat door, Dad would say "Elvis has left the building".

*Maria was a short-haired tabby, and had claws like needles. We loved her, though. She now lives in Italy.

*Grenzy: oh, what a name! Eliza's idea: Grenzy was originally Gretel, but Eliza had a habit of changing animals' names, and Grenzy was in the wrong place at the wrong time. She still lives with us. I've had her for half of my life.

*Demeter: Mum named her. Demeter was tabby, short haired, and had the most beautiful eyes.

Then we got Henry, from an animal rescue centre. He had black fur, but he had a little white smudge on his neck. He would sleep right in the middle of Eliza's bed, and Eliza had to sleep up against the wall. According to The Book of Baby Names, Henry means "King of the house". He certainly lived up to his name. He abdicated, and found another family to live with!

William was the next cat. He'd never consider running away, due to lack of brain. He's a short-haired Persian, though his fur seems very long, and thick, and is technically gingery tabby, but on his "Pedigree Form" (a few papers confirming that he is a pedigree), he's stated as a red British short hair.

Comparisons

Here are several differences between school and home school:

1). In school, we wore uniforms; at home, I wear jeans and tee-shirts.

2). At the primary school that I attended, there were two lunch sittings: First Sitting ~ for school lunches; and Second Sitting ~ for packed lunches. Most of my friends ate school dinners, and I ate a packed lunch, so I only saw them for fifteen minutes at morning break, and in class.

3). At home, there are no timetables.

4). If you really need a moment of quiet time, you can have it ~ if you're at home.

5). Lots of people believe that it's best to have a fully rounded education ~ and I'm not necessarily disagreeing with that; but some people are immensely gifted in some subjects, but know nothing at all about others. If a particular subject won't help a person with what they intend to do with their life, then they shouldn't have to do it (unless they want to). That person should be able to concentrate on the one, two, or however many things that they *want* to do.

6). You shouldn't have to do GCSEs if you don't want to. If home educated, you do still have the option of exams, but they aren't compulsory.

General life views

When I write, I listen to all sorts of music, including *Muse, My Chemical Romance, Paramore,* and many others. It's a strange mixture, as I play mainly jazz and classical on the piano and violin. I had never felt the need to listen to some of the above bands, but some of my friends were very rightly obsessed, and insisted that I should listen to some particular songs. I listened, fell in love, and never looked back. I'm listening to them now. I owe my friends, big time.

In some of their songs, these bands talk (sing) about being con-trolled, forced, being made into "sheep", etc. They are ~ step by step, song by song ~ getting it into their listeners' heads that their schools, workplaces, etc., aren't looking after them, and that they don't care about their future, or about them: they ~ the teachers, bosses, etc., are making them, the listeners, into sheep who can be increasingly monitored, tracked, and controlled . . .

The bands may not know it ~ I don't know, because, sadly, I've never met them ~ but they're right. More right than they could ever imagine!

I don't regret leaving school. I would never return to that sort of school. I miss having my friends around, sure, but I wouldn't go back.

Thank you ever so much for reading the ramblings of a thirteen-and-three-quarter-year-old girl.

Bethany and William having a snuggle.
Opposite page: Paul playing Bethany the guitar, aged 12 months.
Bethany, at 13, playing guitar.

Bethany first learning violin, aged 9; playing violin, aged 13, in the Autumn, 2009.

Bethany's violin composition for grade three.

The Storm

B. A. Robinson

Part Six
by Veronika Sophia Robinson

Auckland, 1997: Pumpkin riding with big sister,
Hannah. Bethany and the big pumpkin!

Autumn

When the girls were much younger, we picked crab apples to make jelly. What a fiddly job! Now we prefer to use crab apples as decorations on our Autumn wreaths. We add bunches of rosehips, too. Is Autumn a time of golden sunshine against rusty coloured leaves, or a season which warns us of impending violent storms? Do we rug up to bring in the first loads of firewood for the season, batten down the hatches, or plant Autumn garlic?

Cumbria's Knitting Café

Tucked upstairs in Bluebell bookshop, is a gathering of women passionate about knitting. Bethany and Eliza first started going to the Knitting café quite a few years ago, and from these women they've learnt different styles of knitting and crochet. It's a social atmosphere of cardigans, scarves, knitting for charity, hot chocolate and raspberry scones! The specialist yarn shop in the arcade features handmade threads from women's cooperatives throughout the world, as well as ecologically-friendly knitting needles made from bamboo and other sustainable woods. So the girls knit with the women, while Paul and I sit nearby working on the editing and proof reading of The Mother magazine.

The Autumn Altar

Acorns, conkers, apples, pumpkins, rosehips, blackberries, golden sycamore leaves and crab apples line our Autumn altar each year. We give thanks for the harvest, and abundance in our lives.

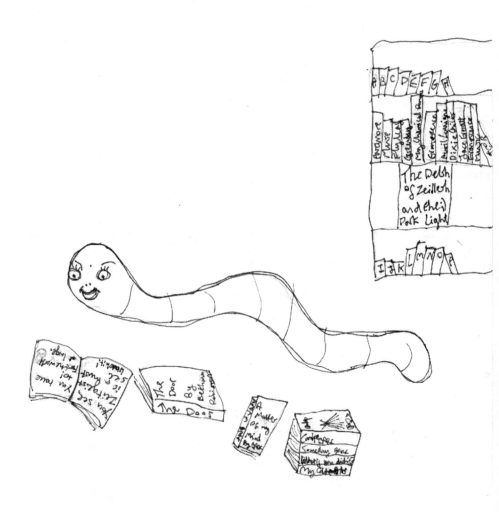

Bethany's Bookworm

Bookworms

I've just tucked Eliza into bed, and had a little chuckle to myself at the five books on her bedside table. From *Child of the Dawn*, a metaphysical allegory, to *I, Coriander*, historical fiction, I know all the books are 'on the go' and being read simultaneously. She's just like her mother! Her father, on the other hand, wouldn't dream of doing something so promiscuous as to read more than one book at a time.

While it's true to say that the girls are avid readers at all times of the year, Autumn signals the start of long, lazy mornings in bed wrapped around the pages of a novel. Brrrrrrrrm brrrrrrrrm chugs the school bus past their bedroom window… and the girls turn the pages of their books.

It's been estimated that it takes a school child about one thousand hours to learn to read and write, and a home educated child learns in about one hundred hours.

I've no idea how I could even measure the amount of time it took for my girls to read and write. It seemed to us that one day we were reading to them, the next they were asking 'what's that word?'. The next week they were reading beginners' books, and a week or two later they were reading novels. Both of them were about seven when they learnt to read, and writing happened simultaneously. It was instigated by them and their questions, rather than by Paul or I saying 'write the letter A'. They would ask, "How do you write the word rabbit?" We'd write the word, and then they'd try it.

They've grown up with an amazing independent bookshop which serves as the most incredible resource to their unschooling life. Not only do they buy books, CDs, music exam books and gift cards from there, but they use the upstairs space for playing the piano, eating lunch, looking up new and interesting facts, and generally 'hanging out' to read and chat at their leisure. Bluebell bookshop is the heart of Penrith, and we've been ever so lucky to be so close to a town with such a special place like this.

Tonight the girls came home from their teenage reading group, held at the local library. The librarian was playing a quiz game, and said they wouldn't do the questions on famous people because no-one would know who they were. He said, "For example, does anyone know who Sir Francis Drake was?" No one knew, except Eliza, who said: "He was an Elizabethan explorer, who led an English fleet in an expedition and defeated the Spanish Armada". Hmmm, amazing what unschooled children know. I thought he was Donald

Duck's grandfather! All I can say is that I'm ever so glad that I'm not responsible for her learning history! Eliza's a walking encyclopaedia, and absorbs all sorts of facts and figures.

I consider stories to be medicine; and as such, we need to be mindful about what influences we introduce to children of such a tender age. As a conscious mother, I've sought out books that weren't based on the Grimm Brothers' fairy tales. Such powerful archetypes tell us important stories about life and life's experiences, but they weren't written for young children. Who are we to scare our youngsters with tales of knives, revenge and evil? There are some brilliant children's publishers, like Barefoot Books and Quest Books, which produce books suitable for developing minds.

Food, food, glorious food

If ever there's a season which conjures up food, it's Autumn: blackberries, apples, pumpkins. Before our meals, we say a blessing of gratitude:

Earth who gives us this food
Sun who makes it ripe and good
Dear Earth, Dear Sun
By you we live
Our loving thanks to you we give

I remember being at a group lunch once, and offering to say grace. After I said this one, a Christian woman was most indignant that I didn't mention God. For us, Divinity (by any other name) is more than inherent in these words. I've often felt that it's a blessing which can be spoken and felt by anyone of any religion or belief system because it reminds us of our connection to how food grows and comes to us. And who's to say that the Sun isn't an aspect of God anyway? We certainly couldn't survive without its Light. The greatest feelings and expressions we can ever offer are those of gratitude and love.

Angel Wings & Feather Walks

This morning, the majority of our culture's children will be inside a building learning about when a King ascended the throne or beheaded his wife, or what some algebraic equation means ~ whether they want to learn that information or not. Meanwhile, my daughters and I are out skipping through Autumn leaves, and collecting angel wings (sycamore seeds). Today we've been on a walk to collect feathers for the Dream Catchers we're making at our unschooling group this week. We'll use willow withies from the garden for the circle, and weave a web with yarn, beads, and tie in dried herbs of sage and rosemary from the garden. This may be one of those examples that doesn't seem like education ~ but if you look closer, what you'll see are children and parents who've had their creativity unleashed.

Our walks in Nature are a time of conversation, reflection, companionship, freedom, fresh air, exercise, exposure to the elements, and spontaneous learning ~ something which can't be measured.

Schooled families have to siphon off bits of time ~ usually weekends ~ to create their so-called quality time. As an unschooling family, every day is precious, and no less so for being quantity time.

It's Autumn. My days often start with my husband bringing me up a cup of nettle tea while I luxuriate in the warmth of our bed. I'll light my bay and rosemary candle, and read for a while. This is my sacred space, my coveted 'me time' ~ something which many parents fear that they'll never again experience if their children are home 24/7. Like anything in life, you have to ask for what you want, and make it happen. If you're with your children all the time, and need some space, find a way to create that in your life. It needn't be for hours at a time ~ even five minutes of intentional solitude can totally rejuvenate body and soul.

On these mornings, the girls will sometimes come and join me in bed for a chat and cuddle at some point. Most days begin with this slow and gentle rhythm.

The family bed has been quite a place of learning over the years. I've not always had the pleasure of a sleep-in. Both girls would wake up ridiculously early, and start with their onslaught of questions. "Mum, what's 2x3?"…"Do you want to do the tables with me?"

As parents who've practised Attachment Parenting, we've chosen to share sleep with our daughters until they decided to move out into their own beds ~ between the ages of five and seven. Attach-

Eliza and Bethany, Autumn in the village ~ 2000.

ment parenting (which includes full-term breastfeeding, wearing a baby in the sling for at least six to nine months, and then some, and sharing sleep) offers a child the opportunities to feel safe, loved and accepted. Our culture has us believing that separating parents from children equates with independence. This isn't true.

I can see how the family bed has extended into the unschooling life. On my bed, we read stories, and we've read divination cards. We've shared secrets, and dreams; we've laughed and cried.

When Bethany had her first Moon bleed, on the Winter solstice, we used the bed to hold a ceremony to honour this initiation into womanhood. She wanted a private ceremony, so I lit the room with candles, and decorated it with red fabrics. For about a year, I'd been adding to her Red Box, a special place for putting in gifts, such as cloth menstrual pads, tea, candles, incense, and menstrual stories.

I shared a menarche story with Bethany, braided her hair, and massaged her feet with scented oils ~ all symbolic acts for honouring her new life. Such a ceremony could equally have happened had she been in school, but would she have embraced it so easily in a culture of tampons, period pains, cervical cancer vaccinations and shame?

Meanwhile, during our ceremony, Paul and Eliza were downstairs, where Eliza was cooking up a 'red theme' feast for the celebration: roast red pepper soup, and tomato and onion salad. Our meal began with Paul proposing a toast to Bethany's entry into womanhood.

Unschooling has enabled us, as a family, to honour our lifestyle, one that many people would consider alternative: attachment parenting, vegan, non-vaccinating.

Blackberries

Blackberries offer high amounts of vitamin C, and if you can eat them raw, straight from the bush, you'll be doing your health a great favour! Of course, they make great crumbles, cordials, and so on, but their health benefits are best enjoyed when eaten raw.

Pumpkins

Eliza's Sweetcorn, Black Bean and Pumpkin Bake

1 pound chopped tomatoes (fresh or bottled)
1 cup sweetcorn
1.5 cups cooked black beans (rinsed well)
3 cloves garlic
1 onion, chopped up finely
1 red pepper
1/2 teaspoon chipotle chilli
1 teaspoon mild chilli powder
1 teaspoon cumin
******

1/2 pumpkin
******

1 cup soya or rice milk (unsweetened)
1/2 cup tamari (wheat-free soy sauce)
3 tablespoons corn flour
1 teaspoon vegan bouillon (or sea salt)
1/2 teaspoon paprika
1 cup tomato juice (you can use the liquid from the chopped tomatoes)

Mix chopped tomatoes, sweetcorn, black beans, garlic, onion, pepper, chipotle chilli, mild chilli powder and cumin. Allow seasonings to marinate the beans and vegetables. Meanwhile, cut the pumpkin into very thin slices.

Preheat the oven to 425F. Lightly grease a baking dish with corn or olive oil. If you prefer a multi-layered bake, choose a deep dish, rather than a shallow one. Lay down some of the pumpkin slices. Top with some of the bean mixture, and keep layering the pumpkin and beans.

Once down, blend one cup of tomato juice with milk, tamari, flour, bouillon and paprika. Slowly pour over the layers of pumpkin and beans, making sure it seeps throughout the whole tray. Cover dish well (with lid or tin foil), and bake for at least half an hour. Remove cover, and bake for a further 30 minutes. Make sure the pumpkin is soft before serving.

Calendula

Every garden can grow calendula ~ those delightful orange flowers. Often called pot marigold, they're from the daisy family. They flower in Summer, and have a very long history of cultivation. It's antiseptic, antifungal, and good for stimulating the liver. Homeopathically, many families use calendula as a salve for cuts and grazes. The petals are gentle, and can be infused for a mouth wash, eye wash, and to soothe the throat. Infuse 2 teaspoonfuls in 250ml of boiling water, and when cooled slightly, use on wounds.

Equinox

The wheel of the year turns again, and we find ourselves celebrating the light of an equally-balanced day and night. The harvest season finds us in a place and space of gratitude for all that's come our way.

18th March, 1949.
Paul, aged six and a half months.

Part Seven

Home Ed Is Where The Hearth Is
by Paul Robinson

Top of page: Paul as an eleven year old schoolboy.
Paul's birthday card, made by Bethany.

These are my thoughts about home education, having decided not to look at what Veronika's written until I've finished my contribution. I bet she's referred to Kahlil Gibrans 'Children', which is a pity, because I'd love to use an excerpt. But, ladies first ~ even Australian ones.

Like many concepts Veronika introduced me to when I was just a young man of 46, home education was a stretch for me at first. But, since it took us a few weeks to get pregnant after our lightning romance, I had a bit of time to digest what the alternative to school might mean.

I'd been married before. My older daughters, Hannah and Harriet were then 19 and 15, respectively. They'd done very well academically, and I'd never given home education a thought; but the light began to dawn in me about doing just that with any more children I might have. After all, I'd read Jean Liedloff's *The Continuum Concept* before I'd met Veronika, and it made a lot of sense to me. In a way, I now see not sending my kids to school as a sort of extension of the Attachment Parenting that Jean's observations spawned. I suppose the concrete things that came into my mind at that time were: not forcing children to be crammed with information before they're vaguely ready; and the continuous bullying I'd endured at school. I can't remember exactly, but, knowing me as I do, I probably thought: 'Well, we'll give it a go, and see what happens.'

My thoughts about the subject go a lot deeper now, and I'll share those with you; but first, I'll tell you some of my background, so as to give you some perspective on why I think as I do.

All parents are home-educators to some extent, just by the example they give their children. What a sobering thought! This is normally the strongest influencing factor in their lives, more so in a home educating family. So, I suppose that Bethany and Eliza's education started many centuries ago, way down the ancestral line. But to keep it simple, I'll keep my great, great, great granddads and nanas out of this, and just give you some insights into my background.

I came into this world in 1948, although people tell me that I could easily pass for someone who was born in 1949. Because I have two comparatively young children as I write this, I like to think I'm a more youthful version of the old codger that I am. When they were little, I used to tell people my girls would either send me to an early grave, or keep me younger than my years. The jury's still out, but spending a lot more time at home with children than is normal in our society must rub off on the parent (he writes, hopefully).

I'm the oldest of four sons of working class parents, from the port of South Shields, at the mouth of the Tyne, in County Durham. When I was five, we relocated to what was then the heavy woollen manufacturing area of West Yorkshire, where my parents could free themselves of family constraints, and further their ambitions to up-grade to business class. If you, too, were born not long after the Second World War, you'll probably remember the famous sketch which was broadcast on a David Frost show, in the 1960s, about class. The actors were John Cleese, Ronnie Barker and Ronnie Corbett! If I re-member correctly, they stood in a line, facing the camera. Cleese, all six feet five of him, was at one end, Corbett, all five feet nothing, at the other ~ with Barker in the middle. It went something like this:

Cleese: (In a posh voice, to Barker) I'm upper class, and I look down on him.

Barker: (In a middling sort of voice) I'm middle class, and I look up to him, and down on him.

Corbett: (In a cockney accent) I know my place!

The sketch was much longer than that ~ but you get the picture. It was very simple, plain, and funny. It summed up how Britain still was, even in the swinging '60s, never mind 1953 when my family moved to Yorkshire. The little town in which I lived was run by a clique of Rotarians, most of whom were also Freemasons, and the plebs found it hard to break in. There was no religion in my boyhood home, although, ironically, my father was a Cemetery and Parks Su-perintendent ~ and so came into frequent contact with ministers of various Christian denominations. I was sent, every Sunday, with my slightly younger brother, to the local Congregationalist chapel. Our parents didn't attend: so it was do as I say, not as I do ~ a trap which most of us seem to fall into from time to time.

Cricket mad, in my teens I began to play for the Chapel team. It was interesting to observe the Sunday piety of the service, and how, six days later, it had worn off, somewhat. I saw quite a bit of cheat-ing, and the occasional threatening of a doddery umpire. It's a good job the next day was Sunday, when all could be forgiven! This was the beginning of my disillusionment with organised religion (as op-posed to spirituality).

My education was straight down the middle. Before going to Yorkshire, my parents sent me to a little private school. How they afforded it, I can't imagine. When we moved, I attended an infants' school, until age 7; a junior school, until I was nearly 11; and a grammar school, until I was 18.

A few years ago, an aunt sent me a letter, dated 1953. She must have found it in my mother's effects, after she'd died. I cherish this letter, partly because of the description of the five year old me, but mainly because it illustrates that, essentially, my personality has hardly changed over all these years.

The junior school I went to had the usual mixed bag of teachers. I don't look back on any of them with a great deal of fondness. I suppose they were blundering their way through life, as most of us do. I remember, when I was in standard 4 (the last year at junior school), there was a boy who was a vegetarian. I'd never heard of that! Obviously, the teacher hadn't, either. One day, after we'd finished the first course of school lunch, she told him off for leaving some bacon at the side of his plate. He said: 'But I'm a vegetarian, Miss.' Her reply was: 'Eat it up, lad. Bacon's not meat!'

I was one of the brighter kids in the class. We would have tests, and (I recoil when I remember this) the person who scored the highest mark would be told to stand on their chair (top of the class!). Then the pupil with the second highest mark would have to stand up, and so on ~ all the way to poor old number 33. My Dad left school when he was 13. That would have been 1935, in the depression years. He had to leave, because his family needed the income. It was something of which he was deeply ashamed. When he shared this with me, when I was a young adult, he'd never told another soul (apart from, I assume, my Mother). I normally was the third or fourth person to stand on my classroom chair; but once, when maybe all the planets were lined up in my favour, Janet Dennis and Robert Gomersall had to wait their turn. I was top of the class. I was pleased for myself ~ but even happier because I'd pleased my Dad. He was just about turning cartwheels. He was living his lack of education through me, and, unwittingly, inflicting a huge burden of expectation. Status was important to my parents, and if I was a star pupil, in my Dad's eyes that would confer a high status on him, and suggest a high status could be achieved by me when I became an adult.

In my last year at junior school I sat the 11 Plus exam ~ which seems ironic, I was only 10. But there you go! I passed it, and went to Heckmondwike Grammar School. My Dad was ecstatic. The school motto was nil sine labore: nothing without work (or no sign of la-

Lynhurst School
241, Sunderland Rd.
So Shields.
5th Jan. 1954

Dear Mrs. Robinson,
                    A Happy New
Year to you all and I hope you'll
all be happy in new Home, Work
and School.
            I was so sorry not to
have a word with you at the end
of term — I expect by now you
are away. I wished to say how very
much we enjoyed having Paul, &
how sorry we are to lose him

            Paul is a lovely boy.
Always the same no matter
if he was 1st out of a game or
last. He is is intelligent and

full of initiative.

His very first morning at
school he found a block on the
floor. He picked it up, went to
the shelf and found the right box
& put it away!! I saw this myself.
Not a word before or after expecting
praise. He was like that in all
things. Paul was so happy in school.
Took everything in his stride.
He has a keen sense of humour.

We hope that Paul will do
well and be happy in his
new school. The children too
will be sorry he is not coming
back. Miss Humphrey joins with
me in kindest regards to all.
Yours sincerely, Edith Stagg.

Bethany, Paul and Eliza, Torquay beach, Christmas, 2009
Paul and Bethany, 1997, having a picnic at the beach, New Zealand.

bour, as one wag translated it). This was quite apt for my personality; elbow grease is the word. They put me in the top stream. My dad was delirious; but reality set in. There was competition from all the junior schools in the area. Janet Dennis and Robert Gomersall flourished, but I didn't. Thank goodness we didn't have to stand on chairs there (I never did have a head for heights), because I was down at the bottom of the table. Relegation loomed, and at the end of the year I was informed that I was no longer in the Premiership.

But, back to the junior school, and the 11 Plus. We were streamed into A and B, even at that age. Maybe 10 of us in the A stream made it to the grammar school. The rest of the class, and all the B stream, went to what was termed a secondary modern ~ where, at that time, there was no way for those children to take the exams we had access to at grammar school.

In the second year at grammar, the streaming was 2L, 2A, 2B. So it was 2A for me. We never did find out what the L stood for in the top stream. My friend Tony's theory was that letters stood for 2 Latin, 2 Arithmetic, Too Bad. As far as the B stream was concerned, he wasn't far off the mark. Most of the kids weren't suited to the grammar school style of learning and teaching. The curriculum and environment didn't cater for their abilities ~ rather, they were regarded as misfits.

I suppose the teaching style wasn't right for me, either. As I progressed through the school, it became clear that in some subjects I was very capable and perceptive; but wherever rote learning and the easy retention of facts were concerned, I struggled. I still do. So I was one of those pupils who could shine brightly in class, but not in exams.

Gradually, my parents came to realise and accept that I wasn't going to set the academic world on fire; and, as often happens in families, the expectations for the younger siblings were more realistic, and set a bit lower.

The grammar school was run in an authoritarian manner. In other words, it was fear-driven. The boys were always addressed by their surnames (the girls by their first names). Within earshot of pupils, the headmaster referred to the teachers as Mr./Miss/Mrs. So And So. But on the odd occasion I heard him speak to a male teacher when he thought there were no pupils around, he addressed them by their surnames, as he would a pupil. I found this distasteful.

My overriding memory of school, particularly grammar school, was the lack of love and intimacy. I wouldn't have described it like that at the time, but that's how I'd express it now. Class sizes were quite large ~ in the 30s. Certainly, it was easy for a boy or girl to get lost in that system. If there must be schools, then I believe there should be within them an ethos which could be regarded as an extension of attachment parenting, up to and including the secondary level ~ in the same way that *home* education can be an extension of that. Safeness and a sense of belonging lead to self-confidence, which increases as more milestones are reached. All pupils should be loved, cherished and respected. There was no sense of community in the school I went to. The headmaster's attitude to his staff and pupils permeated all relationships.

Bullying was common. I'd been bullied at junior school, too. (I can't remember if it happened at the infants' school I attended in Yorkshire.) I was a soft-hearted boy, which made me a target straight away. I've been very empathetic for as long as I can remember, but empathy involves being open and dropping one's guard ~ and for some of my schoolmates that was an invitation to abuse my good nature. In addition, I spoke differently to the other kids ~ so I stuck out like a sore thumb. I had a Tyneside accent, and they had Yorkshire ones. I remember, when I was five, one boy walking past the bottom of our garden. He shouted: 'Oi, kid. Is tha a foreigner?'

When I was about eight years old, as I was walking down the street with my Dad, we bumped into the headmaster. From my perspective, he was a tall, old, rather intimidating figure. My Dad said hello, and mentioned the taunting and occasional physical violence I endured at his school. His response was to look down at me, and say: "We don't 'ave bullyin' at our school. Do we lad?" Suitably intimidated, I weakly agreed with him. Apart from making my Dad seem foolish, that disgraceful handling of the situation led me to realise that I was, essentially, stuck with it. From that realisation developed my later perception that authorities are generally more concerned with covering their backsides than with fairness, even-handedness, compassion, love, and so on.

At grammar school, I was teased, threatened, and occasionally hit, until I was about 16. I tried to ingratiate myself with my peers by making them laugh. As an anti-bullying tactic, it didn't work very well. Maybe I needed a scriptwriter ~ although, I'm still quite proud of this, in my first year...

Q: What was the average fuel consumption of the Spanish Armada? A: 30 miles to the galleon.

In the following year, in woodwork, we were supposed to be making coffee tables. Mr. Brooke (who used to give us a whack on the backside with a piece of 3 by 1 if we forgot our aprons) gathered us round. "Now then lads! Thompson 'ere wants to make 'is table with a round top. 'Ow do you think 'e'd go about that?" To which I replied: "Use a circular saw."

Not bad for aged 12, but it didn't stop the threats and aggression. As well, I was targeted by a gang of boys from the secondary modern up the road. That also went on until I was about 16, when I caught up with them one by one, and beat the living daylights out of them. It's not a course I'd recommend, but after eight years of looking over my shoulder, there was a certain satisfaction. Bullying is really a cry for love, a reaction to deep-seated fear. It can have devastating effects on the victims. I'm positive that it contributed to the underlying anxiety levels which have been a part of my life. It certainly was a factor in my part in choosing home education for Bethany and Eliza.

The teaching standards at the grammar school varied. I think most of the masters and mistresses did quite a good job, considering the constraints they were up against ~ the authoritarian regime, and those large class sizes. The ones who enjoyed most success were those who could blend a certain strictness, with humour. Any good-natured wittiness provided a glimmer of the love that was sorely lacking in the place. I remember a fourth form boy who'd come into possession of an art magazine. It was full of naked women, artistically and discreetly posed. The master on duty in the playground was Mr. Smithson, the head of biology. His suspicions were aroused by a horde of boys crowding around one lad in particular, who had the magazine in his hand. Mr. Smithson went to the boys, saw what they were looking at, and wordlessly, confiscated it. In class, later that day, he said to the boy concerned: 'Philpott, you seem to be a student of anatomy, what is the function of the pancreas?' He brought the house down. He ran a tight ship, and we knew that he wouldn't stand for any nonsense; but he was capable of being warm: one of the good guys.

I scraped by in most of my GCEs, as they were called then. But, notably, I failed maths. In all, I had five goes at it, but to no avail. Maybe a different teaching style might have helped me, but I got the

Eliza, Paul and Bethany, enjoying a countrywide walk in Cumbria, 2000.

same teacher each time. I've got quite strong opinions about maths. My mental arithmetic is lightning fast, and very accurate. My basic knowledge of geometry and algebra equips me for what I'm likely to encounter in life in general. Why did I have to be saddled with the intricacies of a subject that held no interest for me, or use for me in later life, beyond the basics? I was lucky to head in a direction that didn't require GCE maths ~ but not before (and I tell you this, as a vegan pacifist, with some trepidation and a lot of sheepishness) trying to get into the Sandhurst Military Academy. It seemed quite attractive because of all the sport in the curriculum. Fortunately, a sports injury ~ which would have made the Army liable to pay me a pension if it recurred ~ led them to declare me medically unfit. I must have been mentally unfit to consider it in the first place. I wouldn't have lasted two minutes!

When I left school, I was psychologically and spiritually unaware. My personality was largely formed, but I had no insights into it at all. My prejudices ~ the sum of my personality and experience, went unquestioned by me.

After my rejection by the Army, I put all my cards on the table, and said I wanted to be an actor ~ ironically, an occupation that would have benefited enormously from psychological and spiritual awareness. I spent a year in the real world, labouring in the parks and gardens of a neighbouring town, learning more about human nature. Every workday morning, at the park in which I worked, all of the parks department staff met before the two 'gangs' went off to service the other parks, the cemeteries and council houses in the area. In Winter, a big fire would be lit in the yard. We'd try and keep warm around it until the parks superintendent decided it was time to get to work. It was interesting to watch the tension and fear this little character generated amongst his subordinates ~ particularly the foremen, who always seemed to be jockeying for position, and massaging his ego.

One of the foremen was an offensive bully. He had a man, Tom, on his gang who would now be described as having special needs. He was 6 feet 5 inches tall, a gentle soul, not very strong despite his size; and he had a stammer. Every morning, at morning break time, the gangs would turn up at the park where I worked, for a cup of tea and a sandwich. The foreman would 'take the mickey' out of Tom, and imitate his stammer. I was only 18, and not yet confident enough to confront a large, middle-aged bully. My sense of fair play was sorely troubled. The man I worked with in the park was a shy, eccentric person who rejoiced under the name of Granville Grimwood. I had a lot of time for him. Every morning, he used to bring milk for his tea in an old glass medicine bottle with a cork in it. At morning teatime, the bullying foreman would say: "Granville, 'as t' any milk?" And Granville would reluctantly get his bottle out of his khaki bag. He felt very put upon, but wouldn't say anything to the bully. Eventually, the foreman didn't even ask: he just helped himself. Granville was becoming very stressed about this, so I asked him if he had another bottle, just like the one he brought to work every morning. He had! The next morning, he brought the identical bottle, complete with milk. I brought a bag of Epson Salts. I put enough in that bottle to fix an ox, never mind the foreman. The following morning, when we all congregated around the fire, the foreman was moaning about being up till three in the morning, with the skitters. I don't know who whispered in his ear, but he never went near Granville's bottle again.

When I wasn't dispensing Epsom Salts, I was going to drama classes, and applying to drama schools and colleges ~ eventually auditioning, and being accepted at a college on the outskirts of London, to study to be an actor. Because I'd also end up with a teaching diploma, I had to have at least five GCEs (which I had); but they were wise enough to realise that a maths GCE (which I hadn't) would have no bearing on my abilities as an actor or drama teacher ~ so the lack of a maths qualification was no impediment to my progress.

Drama college was an experience that cried out for self-awareness (and financial know-how) ~ neither of which I was instructed in by my parents, or anybody else. I went into a profession rife with unemployment and insecurity. What was Mr. Anxiety, who had been hamstrung in exams because of a poor rote memory, doing in an environment where confidence and a good memory were essential? We'll never know!

I emigrated to New Zealand, the home country of my first wife; and lived a 'normal' unaware life. There were glimmers of something dawning. I read a few esoteric books, and began to experiment with meditation. When I was 28, I became vegetarian; but nothing much changed in my outlook on the world for a long time.

I didn't really begin to develop any self-awareness until I was in my 40s ~ too late to be of any great benefit to my older daughters. When they were growing girls, they got, for better or worse, an unrefined version of me. Unless there is self-awareness, the parent is likely to repeat the parenting he/she received ~ warts and all. While self-awareness isn't necessarily an antidote to this, there's a good chance that some of one's less balanced traits can be at least modified.

For me, now, the fundamental reason for Bethany and Eliza to be home-educated is so that they won't be indoctrinated into the ways that those who control our society (the banks, big business, governments) would prefer them to follow. We're programmed to be part of the herd, rather than be heard. Compliance is encouraged, awkward questions aren't welcome, informed dissent is discouraged. I don't mean that I expect our children to be separate from society, and not be able to function in it. Far from it! I want them to be able to see it for what it is, and, if they choose, to be able to be in it, but not necessarily of it, or dictated to by it. People who are so minded can make great contributions to a society.

The idea is that conventional schools mould children into relatively passive consumers and workers who don't rock the boat. These schools are a perfect environment in which to lay down tracks for future adults to follow. This has nothing to do with intelligence, and everything to do with conditioning and ideology. I was 46 before I began to question my beliefs and conditioning. Because of my upbringing and my education, I'd come to accept the common worldview that certain authorities ~ doctors, ministers, teachers, judges, cabinet ministers, and others ~ knew more about what was good for me than I did. It was quite a few more years before I came to see that the only authority ultimately to be relied on is the internal one at the core of each person's existence, to which we all have access. To see and know that is to have one's life and existence put into perspective. Any alternative ~ even the believing and trusting in (as opposed to direct experience) this point of view results in the handing of personal power to someone else.

But to have that access to our Essence, we first have to acknowledge that it actually exists, and then we have to find out *how* to access it. The average school is certainly not the place to do that!

Work is generally a continuation of school ~ where the mind and energy are directed into occupations which fill the consciousness, allowing little time, and no encouragement, for introspection. Work, for most of us, is a chore: a way of trying to pay for the life we've been conditioned to believe is the way we should live. Most of us spend our lives like rats on a treadmill. Some treadmills may appear to be more attractive than others ~ but they're treadmills, nevertheless.

The other major factor in keeping the attention occupied (often anaesthetised) is the media: particularly television, and, increasingly, the Internet and computer games. Imagine a day full of school or work, followed by the hypnotic box in the corner of the lounge (and, these days, every other room in the house as well). My woodwork teacher called it the fool's lantern. It was the only thing I ever learned from him. The program being watched is almost irrelevant. The result is always that the attention is snared, and pulled away from any internal focus.

The amount of time spent in front of a screen by adults and children in Western countries is a cause for concern. Over the past few years, I've had an annual, seasonal job as Santa Claus. It can be an amazingly enjoyable thing to do, but one of the downsides is listening to the presents being asked for. I still find it hard to believe the number of games consoles that are requested.

Several times, boys have asked for a Nintendo Wii (which is expensive, and, despite the claims, is another piece of equipment to dull the mind, and remove the child from more rewarding experiences) ~ and then they've asked for games to go with the Nintendo DS and Playstation 3 that they already had. And the parents usually nod approvingly when I look quizzically at them (sometimes I ask the child if they intend going outside next year ~ cue: slightly embarrassed laughter from the parents). I've been asked by many three and four year olds for a Nintendo DS (the parents nod)! And many more ask for a television for their room. I have to restrain myself from giving the parents a piece of my mind about the pernicious effects of excessive screen time, and what televisions and computers can do to a child's mental, emotional and physical health, but, (a) I'd lose my job (get the sack?), and (b) they wouldn't want to hear what I'm saying.

In our society, there's a lot of misplaced love coming from parents. It's quite clear, in most cases, that the parents do love their children ~ they just don't know how to express it appropriately. If it were suggested to them that for Christmas they give their children a box which would dispense doses of harmful radiation, and which would numb their minds for hours at a time, they'd be outraged. (Similarly, if it were recommended that they gave their children a mixture of toxins, by needle, starting when they were babies, and continuing every few weeks or months, right into their teens, what would be those parents' reaction?) What's happened is a dulling of the instincts of loving people. The dulling leads to a lack of interest in questioning their lives, and so to the making of uninformed choices for themselves and those they love.

I'm not suggesting that no television should be watched, nor computers used. But unless the watcher is truly aware ~ in tune with their inner life ~ then those electronic media are likely to be used to excess. Awareness leads to balance, and healthy choices.

When I talk about awareness, the inner life, the Essence, I'm not referring to religion ~ which can be another distraction. Apart from the bigotry that's associated with some aspects of religion, even in its gentler manifestations, there's a tendency to rely on intermediaries or facilitators ~ ministers, shamans, priests, or whatever ~ when trying to access what the religion is pointing towards or hinting at. What I'm talking about is cutting out the middle man, and having direct experience.

The spiritual aspect of life isn't something to be over-emphasised with children. There's a risk of boring the pants off them, and turning them away from it. But if it's there in the family environment, seeds will be sown. Similarly, an understanding of one's personality (and that of others) needs to be dealt with lightly during childhood. But it's good to do some groundwork in this direction, once again to establish the foundations for later in life ~ when these things become more interesting and appropriate. In our family, we've found the Enneagram of Personality Types, amongst other things, to be very useful in gaining insights into our personalities, and those of our children. When I came across this method of getting to know oneself, I suppose the most fundamental insight I gained was to realise that there are nine basic ways that humans can perceive the world (and myriad shades in between those nine). A veil was lifted from my eyes. This simple realisation helped me to grasp why so many people I knew didn't approach life as I did; and why they didn't share all the same values as me; and that their way of looking at life was just as valid as mine. Over the years, Veronika and I have found the Enneagram invaluable in our day-to-day lives. For example, one of our daughters, who will remain anonymous, doesn't function well in the mornings. Getting up and getting started don't usually come easy to her. Knowing that many people of her general personality type have the same trait puts it into perspective for us. We've come to accept that she's not being deliberately ornery or difficult: that's the way she's wired. Another example is a very big difference of opinion that Veronika had with Hannah, my eldest, adult daughter. This was quite some time ago, when she was 19. Because Veronika understood how she functioned in the world, and how Hannah did in her very different way, Veronika was able to apply those insights, and approach the situation in an informed, tactful way ~ which led to it being sorted out fully and amicably.

I could wax lyrical about the Enneagram of Personality Types for pages, but this book isn't about that subject, and there are many other ways of developing self awareness, and gaining insights into how to function in this world: to know what might be our potentials and pitfalls. The Enneagram just happens to be a tool we've used. However it's achieved, self-awareness leads to an increased awareness of others, which can lead to empathy and harmony. This applies particularly in the case of home educated children, who tend to be under our noses (and feet) more than school children. As parents, we have increased opportunities to find out what makes them tick, and, in good time, help them to develop self-awareness themselves, so, increasing their empathy and harmony with others.

I repeat that all of this isn't designed to keep our children away from 'the world', but to better equip them to negotiate the shallows and rapids of it. I talk about empathy and harmony, but they're not always easy to find in the competitive environment most of us inhabit. Even our legal system is adversarial. He who has the best lawyer usually wins. When will they come to their consensus, and get their heads together to try to work out if an accused person is guilty or not ~ rather than to try to score points to impress a magistrate, judge or jury?

So, questioning is one of the core traits I'd like to see my daughters develop. (And just as they learned to read and write in their own time, the same applies to questioning.) It's much easier to go with the flow, and not question the routine of our existence. Anyone who does dare to rock the boat ~ or even talk about alternatives, is quickly branded as weird, or a troublemaker. It's hard work questioning everything in one's environment; and most people don't have the energy for it. It's much simpler to blob out, turn a blind eye, and leave the thinking to somebody else.

Here are some of the things I'd like to see questioned by the time children become young adults:

First and foremost, the fundamental questions from which all others will evolve:

Who or what am I?

Why am I here?

How can I be the best possible version of myself?

How can I help others?

Why is there so much self-serving in politics? (If they really believed in democracy, politicians would rejoice whoever won an election ~ because it would be the will of the people.)

Why don't most people question everything around them?

Why do the news media focus almost always on the negative and the banal?

I'd also like them to look carefully at the following:

Our legal system; our health care; education; banking; big business; defence and armament; our surveillance-ridden society; the lack of transparency amongst the decision makers in our society; tribalism; nationalism ~ and just any other ism they could think of.

Among other things, they could question:

What takes us away from Nature's intentions in relation to health, childbirth and child rearing? (Attachment parenting, full-term breastfeeding, and so on.)

They could look at materialism in our society, and the routine dishonesty of marketing, where half truths and untruths commonly go unchallenged.

And how they can fit their awareness into the society in which they live.

It can be argued that our own children have been brainwashed by Veronika and I into OUR ways. But what we're trying to help them achieve is a mindset where they question everything ~ including OUR worldview.

Children schooled in the traditional way can be lovely, caring, bright, enthusiastic and curious ~ but almost universally, they'll be indoctrinated into the parameters of our society: the questions they ask will rarely lead to them breaking the mould.

And finally, the most intriguing question of all: why do Cumbrian farmers hardly ever pull their tractors over to one side when travelling at 15 mph on country roads?

Fear

I've spoken about the lack of love and the bullying in my schooling. A lack of love suggests fear. Nearly all of humanity lives in fear, including people who have tremendous advantages. Our everyday interactions reveal this. Observe the initial mistrust and lack of confidence between strangers. Try smiling at someone you don't know, and see what response you get. Even people we regard as confident and who bubble with enthusiasm are usually projecting this as a mask ~ it's their particular way of dealing with their fear of life.

In fact, nearly every decision, made by almost everyone, is at some level based on fear. This means that almost every action taken is interwoven with self-interest. It may not always be obvious, but investigation will usually reveal this to be the case. Take politicians as the most obvious example, and work backwards from there. Even what we think of as love relationships, when closely looked at, usually fall into this category.

It's fear which leads us into obsessive competitiveness; tribalism; nationalism; us and them; mine and yours.

Fear leads to stress, overindulgence, abuse, addiction, violence ~ and prison.

And it's fear which leads to war. If the youth of our country were encouraged, from an early age, to question in the way I've outlined, there wouldn't be any armed forces, because our young people would approach their lives in a far different way to how they do at the moment. You can imagine the government's panic at the thought of running out of cannon fodder! No wonder questioning is off limits.

The antidote to fear is self awareness. If you know who you really are, fear falls away.

How it's been for Bethany and Eliza

When we first came to Cumbria, we were blessed to have a lovely family as friends, and examples of how home educating can work. All their four children were older than ours, some of them by quite a few years ~ we could see the full spectrum of ages, from about five to 15. We were very impressed by how the parents went about facilitating their children's interests and activities ~ and how their children were self-motivated and took responsibility for themselves. They went on to take and pass the necessary exams for their particular career ambitions. Those young people definitely had the added

Paul and Eliza saying hello to the roadside Cumbrian ponies.
Bethany, Paul and Eliza resting under the sycamore tree.

self-confidence, self-reliance and maturity that often comes with home education. I'll always hold them up as fine examples of how it can work.

As home educators go, Veronika and I are in the unstructured part of the continuum ~ the free range end, where each child's interests and enthusiasms are what lead their learning, not a curriculum or timetable. Bethany and Eliza have been allowed to learn at their own pace. This freedom is paradoxical, because we're quite firm in other aspects of their lives. We could hardly be described as libertarians (we're not as strict as our parents were, but more so than a lot of others we know). Also, Veronika and I have strong opinions on a wide range of subjects ~ it just happens that one of them is on freedom in learning.

For example, our children were read to a lot from a very early age, so the use of language has been readily absorbed by them. We neither encouraged nor discouraged them from learning to read. Both girls, when they were ready, became very interested, picked up the information and skills amazingly quickly ~ opening up a whole new world of independent learning for them. They were reading novels, history books and so on, within weeks of learning the skill.

Reading to my family is one of my two overriding memories of our early years together. I would sit down, or lie on the floor, and read to Veronika and the girls for, perhaps, an hour, every evening. There was no television in the house in those days, and I was the entertainment. I loved doing it. It was wonderful 'family time', and I'm sure that Bethany and Eliza's interest in reading and writing has come, in part, from that experience. The evening ritual stopped when they were about 8 and 6, when I began work which involved being out in the evenings. Every now and then I think I should start it up again; and, indeed, the girls occasionally read to each other.

The other strong, fond memory is of walking for miles down our local country lanes, talking about what we saw, and anything else that came to mind. That memory is idyllic ~ and rather selective! We can't have walked all day. After all, this is Cumbria, so it would have been raining most of the time! And I was often at work. But as a family, we've been blessed to walk (and talk) freely in Nature. And I think that this, and the lack of a rigid structure, have had a profound (and beneficial) effect on both girls.

Along the way, we've come to realise that our daughters are very different in personality. I'm not sure who is chalk and who is cheese.

But whatever leading, directing or nudging is needed with regards their education and learning, will vary in each case, in order to match or complement their individual approaches and needs. For example, because Eliza's interests are more diverse than Bethany's, and she likes to dabble ~ as she gets older, we'll almost certainly have to help her develop the skills of following through, and completing tasks. But so far, the free, unstructured life they had at 'pre-school' age has continued, with informal learning ~ apart from some French lessons; maths (where, occasionally, I'll suggest they put their focus in that direction); and music practice ~ mainly on the grounds that if we're paying for expensive lessons, then practice is part of the deal. "If you don't want to practise, and just want to play now and again, as the mood takes you, that's fine; but in that case, weekly lessons won't be an option."

Home educating means taking on responsibility ~ not handing one's children's education over to someone else. I experienced the traditional school way of doing things when I was a pupil, and as a father, with my older daughters. At the time, I was, by and large, reasonably happy with their schooling; but I had very little self-awareness, and next to no insights as to what really makes the world tick.

This path isn't always plain sailing. If you live in a sparsely populated country area, there's a heck of a lot of driving to be done to take the children to music, drama, French, or whatever. Financially, it's a challenge. Almost inevitably, home education takes place on one income; and resources are expensive. But where there's a will, there's usually a way. It's often a choice between giving one's children a time-rich life, or a luxury-rich life. It's not unlike the choice presented to first-time mothers. For some, financial constraints make it well nigh impossible for them not to return to work ~ but for others there are options. I used to work with a 35 year old woman who came back to work after maternity leave. She was very upset. So I swallowed hard and plucked up the courage to talk to her about it. She and her husband had earned good money over the years. I suggested to her that his salary was high enough for them to manage, at least for their daughter's first few years, with one car, less luxuries, and no overseas holidays. That, apparently was something they weren't prepared to do ~ so, my sympathy diminished, somewhat. Well, totally, actually. And the social side can be a challenge, too. Other home educators and their children are as far flung as the classes our daughters attend, and there's no guarantee that the kids are going to connect, anyway ~ nor the parents. And if you add the layers of 'alternative' living that we practise ~ vegan, non vaccinating, attachment parenting, full-term breastfeeding, self awareness junky, and so on, the worldview that these stem from doesn't always overlap with that of others, even if they do home educate their children. If the parents do develop a friendship, that increases the chances of the children doing the same. But around these parts, the like-minded are few and far between. So, on the downside, our girls' friends don't live locally.

That's probably the one thing that was an advantage for them when they had their brief foray into school. They had a better chance of developing friendships ~ which they did. Inevitably, since they left school, over time, those friendships have diminished. However, when asked if they'd rather be back at those schools, the answer is always 'No!'

School

Bethany went to school because she wanted to see what it was like. When she first said she wanted to do this, it came as a shock to Veronika and I ~ had we failed her? Should we have sent her there all along? Her going to school had overtones of sleeping with the enemy. But, it was her choice. And when she decided she'd go, it was almost inevitable that Eliza would follow suit ~ after all, they'd been constant companions for her nine years. So Bethany experienced the last term of year six, and the first half term of year seven. Eliza was two years behind that. They managed the school work all right, but once the novelty had worn off, they became disenchanted with most aspects of the place ~ apart from the friendships they'd made. They've described it themselves, and it doesn't seem much different to my own experiences at school. Bullying was evident. We later discovered that some parents had withdrawn their children from one of the schools for that reason. And the head teacher displayed about the same level of awareness and sensitivity that I'd experienced 50 years previously.

Where to from here?

Bethany, being the elder, is the trailblazer. She's starting to broaden her educational focus in order to fulfil her ambitions. She's working more on the subjects in which she needs to be stronger. She's approaching this phase of her education with enthusiasm and purpose. In a way, it's a mirror image of when she learned to read ~ when she was ready; and because she was ready, she absorbed what she needed to like a sponge. This is where home education and traditional education start to come together, when there's a need to focus on certain qualifications for entry into college, university, and so on. And for Eliza, with her curiosity gene, we'll continue to prompt her to do as she's always done, to be excited about the world ~ but every now and again, we'll give her a nudge in the direction of going into things in more depth. Although she's the younger sister, she's been her own person for years. It'll be fascinating to see which direction (or directions) she takes in choosing a career.

Well, I've checked with Veronika; and, although she *is* quoting Kahlil Gibran, it's not the bit I want to use.

I also asked her if she'd told the story of the time I met her great friend, Bluey. He came to our home in Auckland ~ a lovely man. He was in his early 70s, and slightly deaf. After a while, Veronika went to the kitchen and I decided to show Bluey my ventriloquist doll. Intriguingly, Bluey could understand everything the doll said, without repetition, even though lip reading was not an option. (It must have been the doll's high pitched voice.) When Veronika came back into the room she was fascinated by this; but she was flabbergasted by the fact that Bluey was addressing the doll by his first name, even though I hadn't mentioned it. She thought that Bluey had taken his psychic powers to a new level ~ until I pointed out that the doll's name was written across his chest in large block capitals!

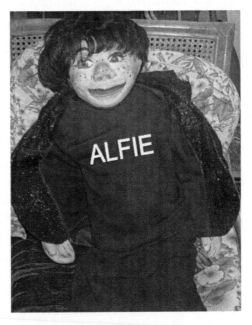

Here are Kahlil Gibran's beautiful, perceptive verses from *The Prophet*:

Children

You may give them your love, but not your thoughts,
For they have their own thoughts.
You may house their bodies, but not their souls,
For their souls dwell in the house of tomorrow, which you cannot
visit, not even in your dreams.
You may strive to be like them,
but seek not to make them like you.
For life goes not backward, nor tarries with yesterday.
You are the bows from which your children as living arrows
are sent forth.
The archer sees the mark upon the path of the infinite,
and He bends you with His might
that His arrows may go swift and far.
Let your bending in the archer's hand be for gladness;
For even as He loves the arrow that flies,
so He loves also the bow that is stable.

Part Eight
by Veronika Sophia Robinson

Winter

Dull sunshine and heavy grey clouds caused me to paint everything bright yellow one Winter after we first arrived here. A decade of English Winters is teaching me that 'light' is internal, and as much as I may curse the grey, dark days, I know that I can bring brightness to any moment ~ simply by choosing to. We can still engage with Nature whether there are snowflakes a-drifting, pewter clouds, January sunshine on frosty paths, or moonlight cascading over the hills.

Winter

A day in our life:

It's mid-December, and it's incredibly mild for this time of the year. I feel myself being drawn to the garden, and wanting to tidy up and prepare vegetable beds! Disturbingly, most of the plants in the garden think it's Spring already. The fruit bushes and trees have green shoots, a flower has come out that's not due till May, and the honeysuckle bush is full of green shoots, too.

8am: The girls are still asleep. Paul's outside cutting wood to make sure we've got enough for the next few days. I'm in the lounge room, snuggled up on the sofa with the hot water bottle, writing my Morning Pages. Afterwards, I wake the girls, and let them know that Dad needs the wood moved to the shed before the rain comes in. They hide under their pillows, but after bribing Eliza with a re-heated hot water bottle, she sits up to do her Morning Pages. Both girls have started this daily practice of flow of consciousness writing (three foolscap pages) to release their creativity. I've found it invaluable, as a writer, for avoiding writer's block.

After we've eaten breakfast, bathed and got dressed, we prepare for the day. For the first time in a while, I've got the opportunity to hang some washing outside. It's a race against time, as I put two loads out and hope they'll dry before the rain. Drying the washing this way, rather than in the Chinese laundry by the fireside, is so much nicer. The last time we took clothes to the laundromat in Winter, most of them burned or melted! It's cured me from going back.

Today's walk is around the block. The block is about three miles up and out the back of the village, around the fields, past the old school, and back in the top of the village. I wonder why there are so many seagulls circling the furrowed fields. We're too far from the beach for them to be here. We walk briskly to get the blood pumping.

The girls spend the whole hour in deep discussion. They want to branch out from the teenage reading group, and also create a Teen Review Group to produce a newsletter/magazine where they can write about the latest books, magazines, movies, CDs, and interview local artists, authors and musicians. They discuss the design, layout, content, reviewers and how to get funding for the publication of the magazine. Business sponsorship or advertising? The conversation veers to where the teenagers should meet up. The merits of all the local cafés are discussed, with the verdict being that Bluebell bookshop is the most 'noise' friendly ~ a requirement for a gathering of teenagers ~ not to mention being comfortable and spacious, and having the option of vegan hot chocolate.

Over the years, many people have asked me if I'm qualified to teach my children. The conversation going on around me right now is ample evidence for allowing children to teach themselves. The enthusiasm in their voices as they plan this adventure is far more creative, inventive and filled with learning opportunities than anything that they'd do in school on an average day. So why do I need to be qualified? Living my life with passion is the greatest qualification I can ever offer them.

I watch the skies darkening over the fells (hills), and wonder if I'll be back in time to get the washing off the line. Our cheeks are rosy red from walking so quickly. Only twice do I interrupt their conversation. When they discuss publication, and that the magazine might be five pages, I let them know that commercial printing is done in multiples of four. In the space of sixty minutes, they've formulated an endeavour that brings together many subjects and interests. They're overjoyed when I suggest that they can contact book publishers, and ask to be put on their review list. Free books! And what about asking the local movie theatre for a reduction in order to write up reviews? Regardless of where this conversation leads, excitement has sparked learning.

We return home, exhausted but satisfied. Fresh air always feels wonderful. Eliza heads upstairs to play the saxophone, and Bethany sits at the piano to compose. I work on a little editing before making some lunch. The girls play Scrabble while I'm in the kitchen. I don't like being in the room with them when they play, as Eliza comes up with words, including slang words, from countries and eras that Bethany's never heard of. It gets fractious!

Eliza's been spurred on by high praise from her music teacher, who came out to see Paul after a recent lesson because she was so thrilled by how much Eliza was achieving during her practices at home. Her composition was at GCSE level. Eliza's managing to do this because she's enjoying what she's learning, rather than because a parent or two is on her case to 'learn'.

Mid afternoon: I light the fire, and the girls start putting their Teen Review ideas onto paper in order to share them with others in their group. There are four aubergines in the fridge which need to be eaten, so I slice them up, salt them, and allow them to sweat for a while.

At the beach in Winter: December 2009, Torquay, Devon.

Bethany's reflecting on the results of her grade four violin exam from last week. She was just three points short of distinction. Surprisingly, she's upbeat, and is looking at the cup half full, rather than empty. She decides that she probably won't do exams now until she's at grade eight level. Eliza starts designing a magazine cover for Teen Review, and Bethany continues her composing at the piano. I use this time to do some proof reading of the magazine, which we've just got back from the printers. The girls then help with some housework ~ cleaning the bathroom, sweeping the stairs, mopping. Taking care of their living environment, and being responsible for their part in it, are as essential to their learning as anything else. One day these girls will be managing their own homes. They help me to rearrange the lounge room, swapping the piano and sofa around. It feels more spacious. Nice. The girls revisit favourite songs from their childhood so that they can teach some young unschooled children in our village. I attend to some administration and emails.

The Sun has set, and the school bus driving by reminds me of how glad I am about our life choices, and relaxed daily rhythm. I hear raindrops. "Quick, let's get the washing in!" Eliza fusses. She's scared there might be rats near the compost heaps. In the end, with a little persuasion and one of the cats for company, she helps Bethany.

I've got some more proof reading to do, but I'm trying to find the balance between my work demands, heading to the kitchen to make moussaka, and being available for the girls should they need or want me. As it happens, they're both quite content and absorbed in their activities. The moussaka, for some reason, reminds me of Winter in 2000, when we were raw fooders. All our meals were raw, and one particular recipe I found for aubergines put me off ever eating them raw again. We still enjoy a high percentage of raw food in our diet (more so when the weather and garden are more conducive), but we also love to cook.

Evening time: we sit by the fire, chat for a while, and sink ourselves into our chosen interests. Paul and I proof read ~ we're under time pressure to get the January/February issue published before the printer shuts for a few weeks over Christmas and January. Bethany's been playing some violin for the first time in a week. She had treated herself to a week's rest after the exam. She and Eliza share some ideas with me for the Christmas concert they're planning. Eliza's got the ukulele on her lap, and is strumming to the cat: a reward for accompanying her to the clothes line in the rain! The incense burns.

Christmas carols play. Another day is over. No uniforms, no lunch boxes to clean, no spelling tests, no tired and grumpy children, no fretting about bullies. Life is good.

Solstice

Heralding the shortest day of the year, we celebrate that the light will return. The Winter Solstice invites us to bring Nature indoors, and our mantlepiece is adorned with holly and ivy from the garden. Green soothes the soul, and every home should have pot plants in to rejuvenate the air. The addition of extra greenery in Winter is uplifting.

Sweet treats

My childhood memories of Christmas include stöllen (German bread ~ fruit loaf with marzipan in the middle) and lebkuchen (spicy biscuits). Lebkuchen are perfect for using as Christmas tree decorations, too, and will last for weeks. Even the cats think they're yummy! Be warned though: cats and lebkuchen swinging from a Christmas tree at the same time are *not* a good combination!

Lebkuchen is traditionally made using honey, but we use agave syrup to save the bees a bit of leg work.

Egg replacer: equivalent of 4 eggs
255g agave syrup
1 teaspoon of pure vanilla extract
½ teaspoon of ground cloves
¼ teaspoon cinnamon
¼ teaspoon ginger
¼ teaspoon nutmeg
1 tablespoon of dark rum
140g finely chopped organic orange and lemon peel
grated rind of 1 lemon
200g ground almonds
100g ground hazelnuts

Mix the egg replacer, agave and vanilla extract together. Add the rest of the ingredients, and mix into a thick paste. If it's too runny, add more ground hazelnuts. Put heaped teaspoons of the mixture on top of baking paper. Bake at 125C for 30 minutes. Bake well in advance to improve its flavour, as it will keep for many weeks. Wrap in foil, and keep in an airtight tin in a cool place.

A vegan Christmas

The highlight of our icy Winter is without doubt our Christmas celebration. Like everything in my family's life, food plays a major role! There can't be many children who get excited by Brussels sprouts, but my girls do. We pack a whole bag full, or two, at the organic market, so we can ensure there are plenty to go around during Christmas week. I think the reason why sprouts have such a bad rap is that they're traditionally overcooked or boiled (yuk). I suggest almost slicing them in half (from the base up), then lightly steaming them. When done, sprinkle a little fresh lemon juice and black pepper on them. Alternatively, slice thinly, and briskly stir-fry with a bit of crushed garlic and sesame oil.

Parsnips and carrots, caramelised in a little oil and agave syrup, cinnamon and nutmeg, and roasted, are mouth watering.

Butternut squash, when roasted with garlic cloves and rosemary leaves, is a meal on its own. Try adding some cauliflower to the roast.

Saddlebacks are large potatoes cut in half, then thinly sliced all the way up the back of the potato, with slits going almost to the flat side ~ like an accordion. This allows them to roast and steam while in the oven. Rub in some Maldon sea salt before cooking, and be generous with the olive oil.

My mother's red cabbage is another food tradition passed from her to me to my girls. Finely slice or grate red cabbage, and fry in a little sunflower oil. Keep stirring. Add a cup of grated apple, pinch of nutmeg, salt and black pepper, and allow it to simmer and steam. Sometimes I add a spoon of apple cider vinegar, too.

Robinsons' celebratory nut roast

225g mixture of cashews, almonds, sunflower and sesame seeds
1 onion
4 T olive oil
100g rice crumbs
1 cup of vegetable bouillon
2 teaspoons tamari
1 teaspoon dried sage
pepper
salt

Sauté chopped onion until clear. Grind the nuts and seeds, then combine with the rice crumbs. Heat the bouillon and tamari, and mix everything together.

Place into a greased baking tray, and bake for half an hour at 180C. If you're feeling adventurous, you can make a sage and onion stuffing using rice crumbs, dried onion, dried or fresh sage, and pressed in between two layers of nut roast.

We always make enough of everything so that we can have this meal again the next day ~ cold. It's just as lovely then!

We Three Kings

My girls know that the three kings of Christian nativity scenes are actually a constellation in the sky.

Each year that we've lived in this village, they've taken part in the village Nativity play at the local chapel. Regardless of whether or not one shares the Christian belief, there's something rather beautiful and holy about sitting in an old chapel with candles alight, snowflakes falling, and cherubic children singing *Away in a Manger*. It's enough to melt most people's hearts. Over the years, they've played every character, and when Bethany was the virgin Mary, she gave the chapel congregation the first ever vaginal birth of Jesus. Stand, squat and deliver! Well, what do you expect from a girl raised in a home that promotes natural birthing?

As with Easter, I've offered my daughters a metaphysical interpretation of the creation story from early on. It goes like this: Joseph is a carpenter, who represents the male energy of 'thinking'. Mary, the young virgin, is pure feeling, that is, she represents the feminine energy.

Though we're told that they'd not had sexual intercourse, their union, as a couple, was blessed by Divinity, and led to the birth of the baby Jesus. The Christ represents our creative self. Thought on its own does not produce. Feeling on its own does not produce. Bringing thought and feeling together is a great creative act that brings light to our self, and to the world. The Christmas story is that of our ability to create.

Coughs and Sneezes

I still remember the smell of Vicks Vapour Rub from my childhood, and all the feel-good associations of mother-nurture. I don't use this on my children, though, due to the petrochemicals in it. Instead, I turn to Mother Nature, and massage with a carrier of almond oil, and add drops of the pure essential oils of eucalyptus, tea tree (both are antiseptic) and lavender (to relax). Eucalyptus oil is also sprinkled onto pillow cases and pyjamas, and added to the oil burner.

We tend to avoid commercial cough and cold remedies in the house. What we do have are essential oils, and teas such as starflower; and the sage growing in the garden is made into a tisane. If coughs linger, we use homeopathy, such as Drosera or Ant. tart.

Sledging in the village, 1999.
Below: Eliza, Winter, January 2010

Toboggan

The beauty of living in a small village is that when the snow falls, the roads are relatively safe for sledging on. There are hills and fields all around for doubling up on the toboggan. If the snow's heavy enough, the school children will get to stay home too, but as un-schooled children Bethany and Eliza don't need anyone's permission to go tobogganing or building snow women!

Rye and caraway sourdough bread

Caraway is an aromatic relative of the carrot. It grows in upland pastures and hay meadows, and is used as a herb. The seeds are antiseptic, and are useful for children who have worms. It's very much a herb from the central European countries, as it's used in goulash, sauerkraut, rye bread and pickles. The stems and leaves can be used in salads and soups.

Got windy children? Infuse one teaspoon of crushed seeds in a cup of hot water. Offer your child up to three cups a day. If you've got a windy husband, it'll work for him too!

250ml sourdough starter
500g rye flour
500ml warm water
Teaspoon of sea salt (Maldon)

The night before you wish to bake the bread, mix the sourdough starter with 250g rye flour and all the water. Mix well, and leave overnight.

The mixture should bubble a bit overnight. Add flour, and mix well. Take a little out, and put into the fridge (covered) for your next starter.

Add the salt and remaining flour. Bake the bread in two small tins, but allow the dough to rise for a few hours until it doubles in volume. Sprinkle caraway seeds on top. Bake for 40 minutes at 180C. Rye bread will keep for a few weeks if kept in a wooden or ceramic bread box.

A Snowy Day

Last Winter, Britain was brought to a standstill when snow fell for a few days in a row. The cost to the economy was, apparently, in the millions, as people stayed off work, and Heaven forbid, went sledging! Couldn't have adults having fun now, could we?

I love waking up on a snowy morning, and hearing the school children crunch their way on icy roads, in the dark, to the village bus shelter. Knowing that we can get out of our warm beds when we feel like doing so is a real perk of our unschooling lifestyle. There's no urgency, no stress to get uniforms on and lunches packed ~ none at all. At some point, the fire will be lit, incense will burn, and music will welcome the new day.

There may be porridge or quinoa on the stove top, cinnamon and vanilla scenting the air, possibly preceded with a freshly made green vegetable juice. A cup of nettle or rosehip tea may be taken, peacefully, and perhaps followed by some gentle yoga asanas by the fire.

Others in the family may stay in bed, and read for some time. The day is ours, the season is ours, and we dance to her rhythm, her song ~ whether it's a walk in the snow to make snow angels, to feed seeds to the Winter birds, or to snuggle up on the sofa for stories and music.

It's early January, 2010, and the country is in the grip of the coldest weather in thirty years. Ten thousand schools are closed, and there's panic in the news broadcasts about children missing out on their education, and if it's even possible that school children can make up this 'lost time'. Such a belief is typical of how little this culture understands about the way children learn.

We've had weeks of snow here in Cumbria, with another week or two forecast to come. Have my children "stopped learning" because of this weather? No. As I type, they're a couple of hundred metres away at the home of another unschooling family in the village. One of the young children in that home received a violin, and another, a ukelele for Christmas. Beside the warmth of the woodstove, Bethany and Eliza are teaching them the basics of their instruments.

Suitcases

Winter is a time to pack away all the Summer clothes, and get rid of those which no longer fit. We've a choice of charity shops to gift our pre-loved clothes. It's fun to rediscover 'new' clothes next Spring; what fits, what doesn't. The funny thing is that whenever we do a clothing clear out, almost to the day, a parcel arrives from a friend down South. She gifts us with the most delightful clothing and accessories in hemp and cotton, and colours fit for a fairy princess. My girls spent their childhoods dressing up, and most of the time there seemed to be very little boundary between day clothes and fantasy clothes. Dressing up was integral to their play time.

Packing away things of the past into suitcases is also symbolic of our changing lives. What works for us one year, or season, may not be suitable the next year. We grow, we change, we move on, we let go, and we make room for the new to come into our lives.

Aromatherapy

Winter is a time for massages by the fireside. Using quality essential oils, in a base oil of almond or grape, the human necessity for touch is satisfied by loving hands which take the time to ease away tensions.

Lavender oil is relaxing, eases tension, depression, tiredness, and warms the spirits.

Lemon oil boosts circulation, is stimulating, and helps to clear colds and exhaustion.

Eucalyptus oil is my first choice for colds, coughs, flu, fever and sinusitis. Use it to soothe pains, aches, sprains, and to help heal cuts.

Jasmine oil is good for postnatal depression, and helps to lift the spirits in general. It's valued for its ability to ease pre-menstrual tension.

There are many essential oils which can be used for massage, in baths, oil burners, to sprinkle on bedding. Our sense of smell is often neglected, but in a loving home it's well nurtured through delicious foods, flowers, oils, incenses, wood on the open fire, fresh linen, air-dried clothes, and household products free from chemicals. Plastic toys which emit toxins are avoided.

When Bethany went for her first evening visit to secondary school, we were given a tour of the rooms. The science laboratory had the most overbearing, noxious odour from having just been 'cleaned'. I nearly gagged with the effect it had on me. When I commented to the teacher about how toxic it was, she said, dismissively, 'the smell will be gone in the morning'. The fumes may have dissipated by then, but the effects of the chemicals would still be there to *poison* the children. And these toxins were added to the room every day. As unschoolers, many things about our lives change. Becoming more aware of the environment, both locally and globally, is inevitable. So is learning to speak up and protecting our children from dangers.

Winter mornings

The local primary school that my daughters attended ~ Langwathby Primary School ~ doesn't let the children through the doors until 9am. This means that all the students who arrive earlier than that, such as the bus students, are forced to stand outside regardless of the weather conditions or if they need the toilet. I was reminded of this the other day, in the first week of December, when I saw them all piled up outside, shivering against the icy winds which had blown down from the snow-covered fells. This amplified for me that there's very little respect shown to school children. Where are the teachers? In the cosy, warm staff room, lounging back on the sofa, and sipping piping hot coffee! Bethany's ex-High School forbids students going to the toilet during lesson time. As she rightly pointed out, what if you don't need to go to the toilet in break time?

New Year's Eve

10, 9, 8, 7, 6, 5, 4, 3, 2, 1 HAPPY NEW YEAR!

When I think of New Year's Eve, I know the odds are high that Paul won't be with us ~ he'll be singing at a local pub, and entertaining the villagers. The girls and I celebrate by having a phoenix ceremony. This involves writing down all the things in our life we want to get rid of, and burning them in the fire. We then write all the good things we'd like to fill our lives with. Sometimes we write our wishes on paper, and bury them into Mother Earth before the clock strikes midnight.

All who were born in January skip around

The tradition for Eliza's birthday ~ apart from chocolate cake ~ is to sing "all who were born in January skip around". This is a delightful folk song from Trinidad. Of course, you can simply change the month to suit any time of the year, but in our home it's Eliza's birthday song. She's now started a tradition of ensuring we go away, as a birthday treat.

All who were born in January skip around
All who were born in January skip around
Tra la, la la la la la, tra la la la la la la
All who were born in January skip around.

Everyone up VERY bright and early for Eliza's birthday on a chilly Winter's morning.

The day of love

St Valentine's Day is one of the most prosperous times of the commercial calendar, as lovers and admirers splurge on chocolate and flowers.

Paul and I don't celebrate St Valentine's Day, but we do honour our private anniversaries of the heart: the day we first kissed, April 16th, 1995, and the day we married, December 29th, 1996. As it happens, Paul and I moved in together straight away. We 'just knew'. For us, every day is a day of love. We don't reserve our affection (physical or spoken) for special days only. As for flowers and chocolates, why save them for one or two days a year? My theory is that if you're going to eat chocolate, eat good chocolate; and so I'll buy myself Booja Booja when I feel like it, not when the calendar suggests someone else should buy it for me. And because I adore flowers, I ensure they're grown liberally amongst my fruits and vegetables.

Modern relationships teach us that it's up to another person to meet our needs. Is that true? Isn't that perhaps our downfall? If we loved and respected ourselves as we expect another to love us, then our relationships would transform before our very eyes.

When I was a single woman, each night I'd set the table with care for my home-made meal, light a candle, put on some romantic music, and dine in the pleasure of my own company. Many women wait years and years for someone to eat with them by candlelight. Candles, flowers, chocolate, bubble baths... we're on a fast track path to misery if we wait for others to bring these little goodies into our life. The greatest romance you can ever have is with yourself. I hope my daughters have learned this from me.

I believe that the love between a child's parents is the true home of the child. Surely that's worth celebrating every day of the year, and not just on February 14th?

Romeo and Juliet   20/01/08   B.A.R.

Bethany's painting of Romeo and Juliet, created when she was eleven.

A Child Learns
author unknown

If a child lives with criticism
She learns to condemn
If a child lives with hostility
She learns to fight
If a child lives with ridicule
She learns to be shy
If a child lives with shame
She learns to feel guilt
If a child lives with tolerance
She learns to be patient
If a child lives with encouragement
She learns confidence
If a child lives with fairness
She learns justice
If a child lives with security
She learns to have faith
If a child lives with approval, she learns to like herself
If a child lives with acceptance and friendship
She learns to find love in the world.

"The best thing to spend on your children is your time."
~ Louise Hart

Go Barefoot

In one of my favourite movies, *PS I Love You*, a young widow is on the verge of making love with a hot young Irishman, when she says "No, I can't do this. It's like trying on a new pair of shoes and they don't fit right."

The hot young Irishman replies, "Try going barefoot for a while." Now, that could be seen as a pretty crafty way around his hormonal urges, but I like to think of it as sage advice. You can do the same if your child is in school, or more structured home education, and you're interested in taking the plunge into unschooling. Stop comparing it to the shoes you're used to walking in. Ditch them, and go barefoot. I promise you'll feel free as a bird, and your family will fly.

What I've learnt since our first visit to Ireland, is that, in fact, we as a family do lots of things every day, it's just that how we perceive what we do has to be re-visioned, especially because culture has such a different vision of what education looks like. I hope you've enjoyed sharing our story.

If you let life be your curriculum, your child will come top of his class ~ always, and in all ways. And remember, Love is the glue… you can't buy that in even the best schools.

Recommended Reading

The Wisdom of the Enneagram: the complete guide to psychological and spiritual growth for the nine personality types *by Don Richard Riso and Russ Hudson*
Personality Types: using the Enneagram for self discovery *by Don Richard Riso and Russ Hudson*
A Call to Brilliance *by Resa Steindel Brown*
Sharing Nature with Children *by Joseph Cornell*
Evolution's End *by Joseph Chilton Pearce*
The Crack in the Cosmic Egg *by Joseph Chilton Pearce*
Magical Child *by Joseph Chilton Pearce*
Magical Child to Magical Teen *by Joseph Chilton Pearce*
The Continuum Concept *by Jean Liedloff*
Learning Without Tears *by Helyn Connerr*
Dumbing us Down: the hidden curriculum of compulsory schooling *by John Taylor Gatto*
Parenting for a Peaceful World *by Robin Grille*
How Children Learn at Home *by Alan Thomas and Harriet Pattison*
Toxic Childhood: how the modern world is damaging our children and what we can do about it *by Sue Palmer*
Detoxing childhood: what parents need to know to raise happy, successful children *by Sue Palmer*
101 things everyone should know about science *by Dia L. Michels and Nathan Levy*
The Potions Club Recipe Collection; from plant to pot to potion *www.potionsclub.com*

About Veronika and Paul

Veronika Sophia Robinson was born and raised in South East Queensland, Australia, the fourth of eight children. She co-founded the *National Waterbirth Trust* (New Zealand) in 1995, with her husband, Paul, and launched *The Mother magazine* to an international readership in 2002. Alongside editing this unique publication on optimal parenting, Veronika's other passions include the day-to-day joys of family life, metaphysics, psychological astrology, organic gardening, living in accord with Nature, self-sufficiency and music appreciation. She's available for mentoring, workshops and talks. Visit www.themothermagazine.co.uk or www.veronikarobinson. com

Paul Robinson was born in North East England, and is the eldest of four brothers. For most of his adult life, he's worked as an entertainer of one sort or another ~ actor, singer, compère, music radio presenter, and ventriloquist. Running parallel to his performing passion is his deep interest in the spiritual aspects of life. He tries to bring those strands together in his relationships with other people. His beloved family would need to be asked as to how far he succeeds.

About Starflower Press

Starflower Press is dedicated to publishing material which lifts the heart, and helps to raise human consciousness to a new level of awareness.

Starflower Press draws its name and inspiration from the olden day herb, Borage (Borago Officinalis), commonly known as Starflower. It is still found in many places, though it's often thought of as a wild flower, rather than a herb.

Starflower is recognisable by its beautiful star-like flowers, which are formed by five petals of intense blue (sometimes it is pink). The unusual blue colour was used in Renaissance paintings. The Biblical meaning of this blue is *heavenly grace*.

Borage, from the Celt borrach, means courage. Throughout history, Starflower has been associated with courage. It's used as a food, tea, tincture and flower essence to bring joy to the heart, and gladden the mind.

Visit www.starflowerpress.com for books, Starflower tea and Starflower Essence.

About The Mother magazine

Each issue of The Mother is gestated and birthed within the walls of our home. Articles are edited, photos and illustrations chosen, and pages are laid out, all against the backdrop of our family life: the simmering of leek and potato soup in the kitchen, great conversations, riotous laughter on the family bed. Throughout the early years, while I edited, my girls would play with cloth dolls by the fireside, a cat would be tucked up on my lap as I typed; a child's fingers made music on a violin or piano; great works of art were painted beside me on the dining room table; and for the first few years, lots of breastfeeding!

The essence of this grass roots approach to a professional publication brings heart and soul to the families around the world who read The Mother.

The purpose of The Mother is not to prescribe a way of parenting, but to help women and men access their deep, intuitive knowing, and find a way to parent optimally. We cover many topics and aspects of natural family living ~ beginning with fertility awareness, conscious conception, peaceful pregnancy and ecstatic birthing. The natural consequences of these are: full-term breastfeeding; the family bed, and bonded family life. We encourage natural immunity and vaccine awareness.

The Mother magazine recognises that modern technology is here to stay, and aims to inform readers about how these can impact on child development.

We encourage deliberately conscious and aware consumerism, including the use of natural products (toys, cleaning and body care). We value and recognise that children learn best in informal, child-led situations. Our articles reflect the value of small schools, forest schools and home education. At times, most of us compromise the optimum, both in terms of parenting, and life in general. We encourage taking responsibility for the outcomes of our choices, actions and inaction.

If you've enjoyed reading *Life Without School*, then we invite you to join The Mother magazine's family. www.themothermagazine.co.uk

Celebrating Eliza's 12th birthday with a trip to Ireland.
Eliza and Bethany in an Irish bog, County Meath, and rugged up
against the chilly Winter.

January 2010. Bethany at the village bus shelter.
"No school for me ~ forever!"

Bethany and Eliza on the ferry as it heads into Belfast port, Northern Ireland.

"Life is an education; it's also a fantastic adventure ~ and all children have the right to enjoy their travels. Afterall, it's their life!"

~ Veronika Robinson